T0137660

On the
Rocks

On the
Rocks

A Storyteller's Memoir

JANE HUGHES GIGNOUX

ON THE ROCKS
A STORYTELLER'S MEMOIR

iUniverse books may be ordered through booksellers or by contacting:

iUniverse
1663 Liberty Drive
Bloomington, IN 47403
www.iuniverse.com
1-800-Authors (1-800-288-4677)

Because of the dynamic nature of the Internet, any web addresses or links contained in this book may have changed since publication and may no longer be valid. The views expressed in this work are solely those of the author and do not necessarily reflect the views of the publisher, and the publisher hereby disclaims any responsibility for them.

ISBN: 978-1-5320-8610-6 (sc)
ISBN: 978-1-5320-8611-3 (e)

Library of Congress Control Number: 2019919776

Print information available on the last page.

iUniverse rev. date: 01/31/2020

To my four children:
Honk, Peggy, Louise, and Paul,
whose creative and dedicated lives
continue to nourish my spirit.

CONTENTS

Preface

A buddy of mine who's well into his nineties, said to me recently, "Why is it I can remember things clearly that happened when I was five years old but I can't for the life of me remember what happened yesterday?" I had no answer to his query but I certainly share his dilemma. The good thing about a memoir is that, being a collection of memories, rather than a full-fledged biography, the author is free to pick and choose which memories to include. *On the Rocks* is a group of stories that have, in various ways, contributed to defining, shaping and enriching my life. Some, as in "Precious Moments", were fleeting and private, but nonetheless memorable. Others, as in "A Trip to Nevada", extended over several days and were shared with three hundred others.

These stories were written over the course of the past fifteen years, many as stand-alone pieces. Only in recent years have I made the attempt to gather them together into a Memoir. A couple of pieces have been previously published in my second book, *An Insistence on Life,* plus a few appeared in various journals.

If, like me, you enjoy exploring, feel free to start reading any chapter that looks intriguing. If you keep at it, the complete story will eventually come together. That's more or less how it's been in the course of my life. Some of the events or periods of my life were, at the time, mighty confusing or worse. My mother's unexpected death the day after Christmas when I was four was certainly both confusing and painful. Only in the second half of my life did that trauma mature sufficiently so that I found myself exploring entirely new, light-filled territory.

Just as the full meaning of the events described in some of these tales only emerged after the "smoke cleared", so to speak, in some cases, it took years for me to appreciate the deeper wisdom that was attached to what at the time seemed accidental, trivial or even shameful.

As I look back over my life, I realize that my ongoing efforts to be a good girl and follow the rules, eventually led to a dead-end, dark place with no easy exit. Finding my way out of that trap and back into the light, required my letting go of all that I cherished most. Literature, history, psychology and theology all assure us that letting go of what we hold dear is the only sure way to reconnect by means of pure love, with no strings attached. While

I'm supremely grateful for my family and friends, as well as the tough learnings I held in my heart, there is still much about this journey that remains a mystery. I look forward to a time when answers to those puzzles may be revealed.

ONE

On the Rocks

It was the summer of 1973. In my forties, I was vacationing in Rhode Island where I had spent my childhood summers on and near the ocean. A dozen friends, some of whom had known one another since those early days, were gathered one sunny afternoon on The Rocks for a swim.

"The Rocks", as we call it, is ocean-front private property with an unusually fine horseshoe shaped swimming spot. Pale gray rocks on the western shore slope down into deep water rushing in from the south until they end at the curve of the horseshoe in a little pebble beach. Continuing around the U, rocks appear again, only here they become "pudding rock"; small round stones imbedded in porous volcanic rock. The arm of the horseshoe ends in a huge chunk of pudding rock we called Elephant. Generations of children can proudly remember the first time they swam to Elephant unassisted.

On this particular afternoon the ocean swells were pounding onto The Rocks with unusual force, hungrily licking the sides as they passed and crashing noisily on the pebble beach fifty yards to our left. After half an hour of sunning and talking with friends, I announced I was going for a swim and asked, "Who'd like to join me?" Paul got to his feet, followed by his children's young baby sitter, Teresa, a native of Spanish Harlem. Paul had introduced me to Teresa earlier when I arrived at The Rocks. We made our way along to the spot where evolution has provided a natural set of steps into the water.

Someone lying lazily in the gentle curve of the rock above us called out a warning to be careful of the surf and undertow. "Don't worry," I shot back over my shoulder, "I have my life-saving certificate with me. I'm very good at the cross-chest carry!" The huge waves subsided for a moment so that Paul, Teresa and I managed to launch ourselves into the water, Paul and I chatting merrily all the while.

Presently I glanced over at Teresa and instantly saw huge dark eyes registering panic. "Are you alright?" I asked. She couldn't even speak but managed to shake her head, no. "Take it easy, I'll give you a hand." I called, swimming towards her. When I reached her, Teresa grabbed me, pushing me under as she tried to climb on top of me, demonstrating the classic behavior of a drowning swimmer. All of the instruction and practice from my life saving course of the previous summer came flooding into my head as I struggled back to the surface. I maneuvered into position behind Teresa and attempted to calm her panic. "Just relax, lie on your back, I'll get you out of the water." My arm went across her chest in a firm grip and I started stroking with the other arm and kicking with my feet for the edge of the rocks, only a few feet away.

Just as we reached the natural steps, a huge wave struck us with all its power. We were first washed high up on the rocks, then swept back out towards open ocean by the undertow. Teresa tried to turn under my grasp and clutch me around the neck. I countered by offering more words of reassurance and tightening my cross-chest grip. Again, I attempted to land. Once more we were knocked down by a wave. I tried a third time with no success. Paul tried to assist by pushing Teresa up onto the rocks, only to find himself plunged under water. He resurfaced murmuring, "Sorry, Teresa." One glance at his face told me he was near panic himself. No help there. I tried again, No go. My arms and legs were aching; my lungs were on fire. My mind and my heart were racing. How long can I keep this up? What shall I do?

Suddenly a calm, clear voice in my head spoke. "You're going to have to let go of her." What? Unthinkable! Incredible! For an instant, I was shocked and stunned. Then, continuing to hold Teresa, I summoned every last ounce of strength and swam back to the rocks, thrust her as high as I could above the water line, calling out, "Hold on!" She was able to grab a hand-hold and crawl up the forty-five-degree incline. Then as the greedy undertow started to suck me back down once more, my hands, knees, and toes, free of their burden at last, clawed at the seaweed and barnacle-covered rocks. Seaweed is as slippery as butter and barnacles have razor sharp edges. The combination is lethal. I managed, however, to cling to what felt like the smallest of crevices and gradually inch my way back to the rocks to where my friends were lying, happily unaware of what had just occurred.

Taking my place among them on the warm rock, fingers, knees and toes bleeding and stinging from the salt water, I felt totally spent and thoroughly dazed. Before collapsing, however, I looked over to see how Teresa was doing. She was lying on a rock nearby with Paul, who had rescued himself in the meantime, attending to her. It would be over twelve years before I was to see and speak to Teresa again.

External calm—Internal chaotic confusion

As I lay in the sun recovering, my mind focused on two items. What was the source of, "You're going to have to let go of her," and how could I have run out of energy and strength so quickly? It took me three years to realize the full meaning of, "You're going to have to let go of her." But the question of my physical stamina I resolved to tackle at once. I liked to think of myself as capable and strong, able to take on and handle whatever came my way. My experience in trying to rescue Teresa, however, forced me to admit I was far from the super woman of my fantasies.

When I returned home two days later, I started running around the field at the top of the hill behind our house in Bedford, NY. For the next three years I got up an hour earlier to run two miles first thing every morning, rain or shine, sleet or snow. I loved it. When

I ran, I felt free, exhilarated, and strangely peaceful. Taking up running was the first in a series of life choices I made in the direction of being more responsible for my health and well-being. Incredible as it now seems, it was several years before I first gave up smoking, then changed my diet, stopped using alcohol, and seriously began to tackle the tough emotional and psychological issues that were poisoning and sapping my energy,

The moment when I came to understand the full meaning of, "You're going to have to let go of her," is hard to pinpoint. I got an inkling three years after the Teresa incident, when I made the first move to extract myself from my marriage. For several years I had been aware that the relationship with my husband was unhealthy and dishonest but I told myself I must continue to pretend all was well for the sake of our four children. During that period, I was fond of flippantly saying, "When you get to the end of your rope, just stretch!" Deep down inside, of course, my pain and rage were building. One day I found myself stretched to the limit, dangling twenty feet in the air. I could no longer put other people first; I had run out of rope and was forced to pay attention to my own condition.

It was two more years, however, before I came to realize the gift in "letting go". I had to let go of almost *everyone* and *everything* I cherished in order to take care of myself. It seems crystal clear in hindsight: living an unhealthy life—physically, emotionally, spiritually—has catastrophic consequences. My experience with Teresa at The Rocks signaled the path my life was to take.

Twelve years later when I saw Teresa at the opening of one of Paul's art shows, she said, "Oh, you're the woman who saved my *life!*"

"No Teresa," I replied, "It was you who saved *my* life!"

The fact is, we were both right.

So, if my "On the Rocks" adventure was the start of an entirely new life, what about the earlier life that preceded it?

TWO

Growing Up in the Close

What was it like being a little girl living on the grounds of a great Gothic cathedral and a boys' choir school in the largest city in the United State during the 1930's? People ask and I have no easy answers. I guess I could say that some of it was great and some of it wasn't. For the most part I didn't question my early surrounding and experiences; I simply accepted life as it came.

A few years ago, while showing two friends around the Cathedral of Saint John the Divine for the first time, one of them turned to me and said, "Jane, after growing up in such an enormous space, it must be hard to have a peak experience!" I had never thought of it in those terms. As a child I simply took the beauty and vastness of the Cathedral and its surroundings for granted; this was the only home I knew. In order to describe my childhood, I need to incorporate some of what I have learned recently, over the past sixteen years. Through working with a variety of healers, therapists and my own spiritual probing, I have uncovered bits and pieces of the truth about what actually happened to me inside the Close so many years ago. Mine is not a story of abuse or depravation; to the casual observer I was surrounded by loving and caring adults. A number of my experiences, however, were deeply confusing and painful, though some of these feelings lay hidden, even from me. Through my recent work, I have come to realize how much of my energy was bound up in keeping all that bad stuff hidden. Bringing it out into the open has been enormously liberating.

Every so often a friend I haven't seen for a while will say, "Jane, have you lost a lot of weight?" It's hard to explain that most of what has been lost cannot be measured on the bathroom scale. In addition to this emotional and psychological uncovering and divestment, I have received various bits of information about the past that have helped me understand and accept the reasons behind certain circumstances and situations in my early life. Though my probings into the dark inevitably relieved my fears, sometimes I was not able to grasp at once the full meaning of all that was revealed. As a result of my journey so far, I am a firm believer in the importance of mystery, while at the same time I am convinced that, as has been said, "The facts are friendly" and every thought, feeling, and action has a purpose. The purpose, when revealed, is never to hurt or punish but always to enlighten and make whole.

From the earliest age, children unconsciously imitate their parents' attitudes and behavior; they pick up subtle signals that tell them what is desirable, possible, and forbidden. After my mother's sudden death when I was four and a half, I no longer had a role model for how to be a female person. I turned to my father to see how I was supposed to behave. What do you do when the center of life is ripped away? What my father did was suppress all signs of grief from the outside world and carry on as though nothing were wrong. So that's what I learned to do; keep my painful thoughts and feelings to myself, only allowing them to escape through my dreams and under the covers at night.

Early Memories

I am on a boat, looking out a window at water. Other boats pass by: a tug pulling a heavily laden barge, a sailboat under power, a cutter with a large wake headed in the opposite direction. My mother is sitting up in a big bed. Why is she in bed on a boat? Boats don't have big beds; they have narrow bunks.

For years I had no idea what this memory was about until one day, as an adult, I realized I was remembering visiting my mother after my brother Dudley's birth at the Doctor's Hospital overlooking the East River in Manhattan. I was two years old. Another scene from that time has me standing in one of the bathrooms in our apartment looking up and watching water splash out of an odd shaped rubberized contraption as my mother worked away diligently with a wash cloth; Dudley was having his first bath. For the next two years most of my memories are of a similarly domestic nature, centered around family and home, most of them innocuous and happy.

Then, quite suddenly, my mother died. A few days before Christmas she was taken by ambulance to St. Luke's Hospital one block away; the diagnosis was pneumonia. The last time I saw her was when my father took my two brothers and me to see her on Christmas Eve. He warned us that we wouldn't be able to see her very well because she was in an oxygen tent but that she could see us. In those ancient days before plastic, oxygen tents were great canvas affairs with small isinglass windows in the front and sides. We stood at the door to her room, Daddy held me up and I saw her face smiling at me. I can still see that face.

The day after Christmas everything changed and nothing changed. I have a vivid memory of my father appearing in the living room of our apartment with Bishop Manning at his side. Seated in the wing chair he gathered the three of us children around him and without any preliminary said, "I have very bad news for you. Your mother is dead." Then he burst into tears. I was more alarmed at seeing my father cry than at his words. What do they mean, I silently wondered? I looked at my six-and-a-half-year-old brother, Jay. He was sobbing. Dudley's great two-year-old blue eyes remained dry. He showed no signs of understanding what had happened but he looked thoroughly frightened. I didn't understand either but I felt a heaviness in our little circle and could see the Bishop's solemn manner as he sat in the chair next to my father. Frightened and confused rather than sad, I forced myself to cry. Bishop Manning said a prayer and there the memory fades. For many years afterwards I felt ashamed of those forced tears.

The meaning of my father's rather blunt announcement soon became apparent. Mummy didn't come back from the hospital. She was no longer there to answer my questions, tell me what to do, read me stories, comfort me when I skinned my knee, and tuck me in at night.

I looked to my father to see how he was coping with this thing called death. He appeared to be carrying on as though nothing were wrong. I decided that was how you were supposed to behave when your mother dies. I only cried when I was under the covers in bed at night. This strategy worked pretty well for over forty years. Then a troubling bit of behavior developed.

In a desperate effort to extract myself from a twenty-year marriage gone sour, I had moved out of my house and was living alone near my younger children's schools in order to see them as much as possible. It was a time of darkness and turmoil. The one person who seemed to understand what I was going through and on whom I could rely for support was a friend named Jack. One day he came to visit and when he left, he drove off without mentioning a future time when we would get together again. I didn't think much of it at the moment his tail lights departed down the drive but after an hour or so I noticed I was feeling anxious. The feelings grew and grew until my entire gut felt as though it were churning with double-edged razor blades. When would I see him again?

Was he ever going to return? When he called the next day, I tried to explain my anxiety but he couldn't understand what I was fussing about. Either could I. So, I did what I had done all my life, I decided that I was being foolish. But those pains had been excruciatingly real.

That evening I lowered myself into a hot bath, still pondering the mystery of why I had become so upset after Jack's casual departure the day before. I lay there soaking and pondering for some time. All at once, with no warning, out of my mouth tumbled, "That's what my mother did! She went away without telling me she wasn't coming back!" Then came the racking tears. Eventually I climbed out of the tub, dried myself and fell into bed totally spent as though I had just run a marathon. At long last a tiny piece of the four-year-old had emerged from under the covers.

Another bit came to light several years later when I was studying human energy fields and spiritual healing with Barbara Brennen, author of *Hands of Light*. Sometimes in class when she would ask a question, my response would be to go into confusion and mumble, "I don't know." At those times I felt miserable, as though I were enveloped in a thick pea-soup fog. Barbara suggested I might be helped by working with an NLP therapist. I was familiar with Neurolinguistic Programing, having previously taken an introductory course. Off I went to the therapist who, by asking a number of questions, was soon able to put me into my miserable state of confusion. While there, she asked, "When was the first time you felt like this?" Much to my surprise, into my mind flashed the scene of my mother's funeral in the Cathedral. Once again came the tears of a frightened child.

Up until that moment, the only memory I could connect with Mummy's funeral was kneeling with my one-day-older-than-me double first cousin, Sally. We were whispering together, absorbed in some kind of game. Afterwards I remember my father scolding me for not behaving properly and me not knowing what I had done wrong. A few years ago, a contemporary of my parents said to me, while speaking about the death of another young mother, "It was the saddest funeral I've ever been to, except for your mother's." Until that moment, I had never thought about how devastated family and friends must have felt at the unexpected death of a vigorous, popular, fun-loving young woman, still in her twenties, and mother of three small children, aged two, four and six.

The effect of being surrounded by so much sadness and grief must have been very scary indeed for the four-year-old, especially since she had no understanding of what it meant to die. No wonder I decided to cover myself in a thick cloak of confusion. Certainly, joining the other mourners and sharing their feelings was unthinkable. No doubt denial seemed infinitely safer. Though I had no way of proving it, I suspect my dyslexia, which surfaced a year later, stems from this moment.

For many months after my mother died, I dreamed about her at night. In one dream she promised she would come back but on the strict condition that I wouldn't talk to her. I eagerly accepted the bargain only to awaken in the morning to reality and feelings of devastating sadness. It was about this time that I started complaining of cold feet in bed at night. My father's solution to this problem was to have my nurse, Kitty, sew up a knitted baby blanket in the shape of a pillow case for me to put my feet in. It didn't help much. My feet still get cold in bed but now I have enough sense to use an electric heating pad.

Perhaps it was when I went off to school the following fall that I first became acutely aware of being "different". Everyone else had a mother except me. They were always there at the end of the school day to fetch their daughters. I had to settle for Kitty. I came to think of myself as though I had one arm missing and that there was a huge ugly scar where the arm had been torn off and that everyone could see it. I felt deeply ashamed of this hideous blemish.

Surroundings

For the first eleven years of my life we lived in a four-room apartment on the second floor of the Cathedral Choir School which my father ran with considerable enthusiasm and a firm hand. It was a boarding school for forty boys between fourth and eighth grades that provided the treble portion of the choir for the Episcopal

Cathedral of St. John the Divine in New York City. The grounds, covering two city blocks and enclosed by a high chain-linked fence, were known as The Close. The only section not fenced off was the main entrance of the cathedral at the northwest corner of the Close. A wide flight of stone steps led directly down onto the public sidewalk running along Amsterdam Avenue. A driveway, just to the south of the cathedral, and parallel to it, ran east past one end of the Bishop's four-story residence, known as the Palace. This imposing mansion was set in the middle of the Close facing Amsterdam Avenue and behind it, connected at a right angle by a sally port, stood the more modest Deanery.

To the left of the drive, opposite the Palace, and tucked up close to the side of the cathedral, as though blown in from another era during a hurricane, was a curiously misshapen brick building painted white with impossibly steep steps leading up to the huge Greek pillared façade. It housed a grab bag of people and activities; the Cathedral shop, the clergy and choir vesting rooms, the maintenance shop, the Close telephone switchboard, various offices and apartments.

Beyond this neo-Greco oddity, the driveway continued east, sloping downhill slightly, flanked on either side by lawn, until, near the eastern end of the Close, it reached the Choir School. This was a long H shaped building, with a walled stone terrace in front, also facing Amsterdam Avenue. There the drive turned right and passed between the school and the Deanery, then split in two directions. One branch curved left around the back of the school, descended a steeper hill and ended on Morningside Drive. The other curved right and continued back out to Amsterdam, passing the Deanery and Bishop's Palace to the right and, to the left, the Deaconesses' House, then finally the Diocesan Offices, attached to the Synod House. All these buildings, four or five stories high, were of the same gothic design (save the simpler deaconess' house) and made of granite with leaded casement windows.

The areas between these massive structures were open lawn, edged with trees and shrubs and crisscrossed with connecting paths. In the middle of the large lawn between the cathedral and the Synod House stood a curious bit of carved yellow stone known as "The Pulpit". It was square in shape, with a six-sided base of three steep steps leading up on all sides to the pulpit. If you stepped inside the three-foot high wall through a stone gate, you could see out in all directions. At the four corners of the pulpit, pillars rose another six feet or so to hold up the carved roof. I used to go there with my brothers to play. At other times it reverted to become the perfect spot for me to declaim important truths to all the world.

In front and to the right of the choir school was a square lawn we considered ours. Nestled in the shadow of the cathedral stood a single swing and nearby a sandbox. My older brother, Jay told me that if I swung high enough, I would go all the way over the top in a complete circle. I pumped and pumped as hard as I could but never quite made it. A narrow path led along the western edge of that lawn, next to the brick building and then turned left and passed between it and the cathedral. There it widened somewhat so that there was space to park several cars. My father kept his little Ford coupe with a rumble seat in one of the slots. We used to ride our tricycles and later, bicycles, along this circular route around the brick building, always peddling as fast as we could when we came to the dark and gloomy place at the back between the cathedral and the brick building; it felt sinister and brimming with unnamed peril.

I remember seeing my first iris blooming in a bed next to the brick building one glorious May day. It was the deep purple variety with rich golden yellow at the center and I thought it was the most amazing and beautiful sight I had ever seen.

Important People

I loved hearing the boys' voices as they practiced in the school choir room. Clear soprano tones would filter up into the nursery or out onto the lawn as I sat playing with my dolls. Even better, I liked to listen to the full choir of men and boys sing in the cathedral where the echo resonated up onto the domed ceiling and then bounced back and penetrated not only my ears but the very pores of my skin until the vibrations reached my bones where they lodged with a satisfying tingle. (Fifty years later I was to experience the same sensation when Barbara Brennen intoned pure sound into my broken arm and chakras while demonstrating in class a technique for healing through sound resonance.) While I wasn't an official member of the school, I used to enjoy taking part in some of its rituals. I remember how I loved walking beside my father each morning from the school over to one of the chapels in the Cathedral for morning prayers with all of the boys marching in double-file ahead of us. Sometimes, much to my delight, Daddy would give me a free ride; that is, I would stand on his polished English brogues as he stepped forward stiff-legged and carried me along holding onto my hands. When we got to the chapel, I went to my own little chair waiting for me near the back where the faculty sat.

It is impossible to say when I first became aware that the Cathedral was the center of everything that happened in the Close. My father, in addition to being headmaster of the Choir School, was Precentor at the Cathedral, overseeing most of the events that took place within its granite walls. At an early age I began to notice that some of the people who came there were distinctly Important. These Important People wore special clothes, long flowing robes of black and white and sometimes crimson. My father was one of the Important People but there was another person who was more important, even though he was small in stature. On special occasions he wore a fancy brocade cloak and a funny hat that came to a point, with two streamers hanging down the back. Sometimes he carried a stenciled and gilt staff, the top of which was elaborately fashioned in gold with sparkling jewels. The voluminous sleeves of his white vestment, peeking out from under the cloak, were made of fine linen, caught at the wrist with a broad band of crimson silk. I learned that this impressive, most important person was called the Bishop and he always came at the end of the procession.

Sometimes huge crowds of people came flooding through the great bronze doors at the west end of the Cathedral. On those occasions, many candles were lighted, everyone dressed in their finest. The procession—including the choir—that marched up and down the aisles was filled with Important People, many of them wearing brightly colored silk and velvet shawls. Years later I discovered these were academic hoods signifying rank and classes of importance. I loved to watch the shawls go by and secretly decide which was the most beautiful. Every time I saw my father's shawl, I got a special thrill. It was made of pale blue silk trimmed with creamy white ermine fur. Only now and then did I spot a shawl that I considered more special. Once in a while, when I went into my father's office in the school, I would see the shawl hanging on the back of the door. Then I would go over and stroke the lovely soft fur and admire the texture of the grosgrain silk.

Of all that went on in the Cathedral, I loved the music and pageantry best. I could tell that the words were important, especially to my father and the other Important People, but I didn't understand much of what was said in those early years. One thing I did understand, however; there was no place in this world for me. All the parts were played by men. In the Choir School, the Cathedral, and in various buildings around the grounds, men held all the positions of power and importance. What's more, visiting dignitaries from afar were all male. I learned that these important men were all doing what was known as "God's work". The reason they were so important was that they had been given special permission by God himself to perform certain rites and be in charge of everyone else and teach them how to be good. God, I learned, was all-loving, all-powerful, and all male.

Exploring

Not only did I go to the Cathedral for services on Sunday and during the week but often after school my father would call me from whatever I was doing to take me off on an adventure. Sometimes we would climb endless spiral stone stairs onto the clerestory balcony. From there I could look down into the Nave where the people below walking about seemed so small. It was from this vantage that I first heard Bach's St. Matthew Passion performed when I was seven years old. My father had reserved a number of seats up there for some of his Gilbert & Sullivan buddies from the Blue Hill Troupe. Even though it was an evening performance, I was allowed to stay up late. One glamorous lady offered to share her libretto with me but I declined, preferring to stand at the stone railing in front and envelope myself in the whole event. For me, this was not about following musical notes on a page; rather it was pure theatre on the grandest scale. Like a sponge, I soaked up the scene; the thunderous, rumbling organ, the orchestra with its many fascinating instruments, (especially the kettle drums with their gently rumble), the huge chorus and brilliant soloists with astonishing voices, the familiar sound of the boys' choir coming from high up at the rear of the Nave, and the endless rows of chairs that were filled with what looked like heads and laps. Who are all these people and where have they come from?

At least once I remember climbing with my father all the way up to the top of the great dome over the crossing. We stepped through a little door onto a narrow circular ledge with a not very secure railing and peered down onto the brick dome in the center. We were above the ceiling! I was both excited and apprehensive. To be so high up! But what if I slipped off the narrow ledge and tumbled down onto the top of the roof? The very thought made my legs feel all rubbery. How would anyone rescue me? High above us towered another angled roof which my father explained was merely temporary. Much of what he tried to teach me about architecture was quite literally over my head but I have retained the thrill of exploring every inch of that great gothic edifice so long ago.

Perhaps the most unusual architectural outing I remember was the day my father took me in a rickety, open construction elevator onto the scaffolding just under the ceiling of the choir. Here we found dusty workmen carving figures into the stone above our heads. Daddy explained to me what they were doing, talked to the stone carvers, and then we descended as we had come.

Many decades later, every December when I attended the Paul Winter Solstice concert in the Cathedral, and I would see the fellow suspended way up over the altar with a great gong, I'd think, "You may high up there, buddy, but I've been even higher!"

Not all my adventures were lofty, however. Sometimes I descended into the depths of the crypt and wandered about in the dim light through a maze of passages, past the massive bases of the granite columns that support the giant building above. Much of this space was empty but who knows what lurked in the shadows? For several years my father arranged for his fellow backstage members of the Blue Hill Troupe to build and store the scenery in the crypt of the Cathedral for the troupe's yearly production of Gilbert & Sullivan operettas. I used to hang out down there on weekends and make myself useful holding saws and hammers and fetching nails. The Troupers were a jolly laughing group who drank beer and munched on sandwiches, quite a contrast to the solemn, dignified goings-on above in the Nave. There were times when the Troupers below were having such a good time that my father had to send a runner down to tell them to be quiet; their hammering, sawing, and voices were filtering up through the heat registers and disturbing the worshippers. At other times Daddy was down there himself, dressed in work clothes, banging nails and sawing away with the rest of the backstagers.

The School

From time to time the Troupe held their regular Sunday evening rehearsals in the Choir School. Since most of the boys were allowed to go home after Evensong on Sunday afternoon, the school was fairly deserted then. I remember sitting with my grandfather, a charter member of the Troupe, in the boys' choir practice room just inside the front door of the school. Grandpa was a bass so we sat high up at the back. Each row of oak benches with straight backs was raised one step above the one in front so that the conductor and the choir could see one another clearly. When the full Troupe chorus let loose in that relatively small space, I could feel my bones tingle. Later on, in the season, staged rehearsals were held in the school dining room while I watched spellbound from the adjoining common room. I remember Captain Corcoran greeting his crew of H.M.S. Pinafore from the long head table on the raised platform at the end of the room. Normally this was where I sat during meals, opposite my father whose place at the center commanded the entire room. Except when the Troupe took over, Daddy was the undisputed "Captain" of his domain.

On the ground floor of the school, the choir room and next to it the study hall, took up one wing of the H configuration. At the other end was the Common Room with a large stone fireplace and glass-covered bookcases along two walls connected by double sliding doors to the dining room, both furnished with sturdy oak tables, chairs, and sofas. Every morning after breakfast when the boys lined up in the Common Room for inspection, I joined the queue. A master stood with his back to a window and checked to see that hair was combed, clothes were neat, shoes polished, teeth brushed, hands and face clean. It was also a time to see if anyone was coming down with a cold, flu or, heaven forbid, the measles. From my place near the back of the line I watched boys frantically engaged in last minute tie straightening, hair combing and shoe polishing. This last was accomplished by standing on one foot, bending the other behind you and rubbing briskly on the back of a knee-sock clad calf. In those days young boys wore short pants until their voices changed.

1940

In the center section of the school ran a long hall with classrooms on the back side, each containing a piano, and offices with windows onto the terrace in the front. My father's office was in the middle opposite a flight of marble stairs leading to the second floor. Opposite the stairs hung a large colored print of Aurora Bringing Forth the Dawn. I thought she was the most beautiful lady imaginable.

Our apartment was over the offices, consisting of my parents' bedroom, a bathroom, our nursery, the living room, another bathroom, the dining room and finally a narrow kitchen. The rest of the second floor was taken up with two long dormitories and masters' apartments at either end with bathrooms in between. I was not allowed in that part of the building but occasionally, when no one was around, I would sneak down to one of the dormitories to explore this male world. Each boy had his own cubicle containing a narrow bed, a bureau, a place to hang his clothes and a foot locker. Pictures from home sat on top of bureaus, model ships or airplanes perched on shelves, here and there a teddy bear could be seen. At the front of the cubicle, a curtain hung from a thick oaken rod and could be pulled for privacy. I wondered what it would be like to live in such a space.

The stairs leading up to the third floor, just outside the door to our apartment, were no longer marble but made of wood that creaked when you stepped on certain treads. The teachers not in charge of dormitories lived on the third floor. The wing over the school Common Room and Dining Room housed the gym. It had a wonderful echo and I liked to go up there by myself and listen to my voice bounce off the walls and high ceiling. For many years I had a recurring dream that took place in that gym. I would flap my arms with elbows bent and with great effort lift off the floor until I was floating around eight feet up at the height of the windows. It was a thrilling sensation but required enormous concentration and all the strength I could muster.

The other wing on the third floor contained the infirmary, a sewing room where I first encountered my mother's sewing machine, which eventually came to me, and several small bedrooms for the school maids and

Kitty. A number of nights I remember climbing the creaky stairs and padding down the hall in bare feet, in search of Kitty because Dudley had awakened and was crying. Sometimes she was in her room and came down to deal with the problem. More than once, however, I remember she wasn't to be found. Making a novena at her church, I was told by one of the maids. Back I went to our nursery to try to console Dudley by fetching a drink of water. As a last resort I would retreat to my bed in the corner and put a pillow over my head to block out the sound of his wails.

Once, when Dudley awoke crying and no one appeared, in desperation I started crying myself. Finally, two of the older choir boys came to the rescue. I did not want to be considered a cry-baby like my brother in front of these "older men", so I hid under the covers, pretending to be asleep. The problem, it turned out, was that Dudley had wet his bed.

One of the boys was Charlie Walker, who grew up to be a fine organist, choirmaster and choral conductor of some note. He took charge of comforting my brother while his partner changed the sheets. I remember peeking through half-closed eye lids to watch Charlie stroll around our nursery with Dudley in his arms, offering soothing words.

At one point they came over to my bed (my eyes were shut tight) and I heard Charlie say, "See, your sister is sleeping soundly like a good girl. Why don't you do the same thing?"

Forty-five years later, Charlie told me, "I knew you weren't really asleep."

The Women in My Life

Once my mother died, I lost my role model of how to be a female person. The only women I saw on a daily basis were either under my father's authority or found grievously wanting by him. My father was nothing if not opinionated and so my early assessments of people, places, and events were colored by his influence. It took me many years to figure out that in some cases he was way off base.

First there was my Irish nurse, Kitty, who had come to us the September before my mother died. She was very good to me and usually understanding but had little power of her own. When I decided to grow my hair and have braids, she was the only one who could brush and braid it without pulling.

When I was being particularly naughty, she would threaten to get her hairbrush but she never did. A more alarming threat was, "If you don't stop at once, I'll have you take yourself downstairs with your chair and sit by the front door 'til your father comes home and then you can tell him why you're there." I would rather have been eaten by lions.

The several maids who worked in the school were also Irish and while I loved to listen to their lilting talk, they too were hardly role models. Then there was Miss Thornton who taught the younger boys. She was a Southerner of indeterminate age, wore a pince-nez, talked in a high nasal voice and was considered faintly ridiculous. Next came my father's secretary, Miss Updike. She was young and pretty and wore flowered dresses. I liked to go into her office where she would let me lick stamps and sometimes help fold and stuff envelopes. I don't think I saw it as my life's work, however. When she left to get married, miraculously she was replaced by her sister, another Miss Updike, who could have been her twin. The school nurse with that amazing little white hat perched on top of her white hair, bustled about in a stiff white starched uniform. Not exactly cozy.

Outside the school walls, in the Close, there were several women whom I encountered from time to time. The various secretaries in offices throughout the grounds always had a smile and seemed glad to see me when I appeared, but they were remote figures behind huge desks piled high with papers. Mrs. Muncaster, the wife of the head of maintenance, took care of us on Kitty's day off. She was an expert with thread and needle, hand sewing tiny dresses, bonnets and undergarments for all my dolls. I remember watching with fascination as she stitched bits of colored fabric together week after week until finally a pattern emerged and it turned into a quilt which for years covered Dudley's bed. Years later, the quilt, after a period of neglect, was finally rescued by my artist daughter, Peggy. She repaired it and now it hangs in her studio where she claims it inspires her amazing multimedia stitched creations.

Another group of women in the Close were what my father referred to as, "those silly deaconesses". The deaconesses lived in a house on the grounds, wore a black habit like nuns but somehow were different. I used to see them bustling back and forth on the path between their house and the cathedral. I don't know what they did with their time except run a Sunday school in the crypt of the Synod house on Sunday mornings, which I enjoyed in spite of my father's scathing comments. In addition to classes, they held a children's service that I liked because I could march around in the procession with the other children and sing songs and take turns playing important parts such as carrying the cross and taking up the collection. Here I didn't feel excluded. I did notice, however, that the deaconesses were not part of the Important People group at the Cathedral; they only flitted about at the edges, like moths on a summer's evening.

Then there was old Mrs. Gates next door in the Deanery, whom I visited occasionally. It seemed as though she never left the chair in her gloomy sitting room where she spent her days pasting used Christmas cards into huge albums that were sent to old people's homes and hospitals to entertain the inmates, in the long-ago days before television. Next to the Deanery, in the Bishop's Palace, Mrs. Manning presided in regal splendor. She was easily a foot taller than the Bishop, walked with a stoop, perhaps to compensate for her height, dressed elegantly in muted shades, and applied a great deal of white powder to her long aristocratic nose.

I did have one buddy in the Close: Aunt Frances, the Mannings' unmarried daughter. She lived in the Palace with her parents and managed the household. She was fun to be around, and had her own large sitting room on the ground floor, called the "Ghost Room", with cupboards full of toys and games. There she served tea every afternoon at four. I loved to go and see Aunt Frances because she didn't mind being silly and always had a new game to play or story to tell. After my mother died, she was the one female adult in my everyday life who really knew how to have fun. One of her favorite tricks was to get us scuffing along the thick carpet in the Ghost Room with our leather-soled shoes on a winter's afternoon and then touch her arm so that we created a spark of static electricity. In my highly prescribed little world, this passed for living dangerously. In warm weather I often found Aunt Frances outside, seated in a reclining canvas chair on the lawn in front of the Palace.

I had a nasty experience with one of those chairs that I shall never forget. The chairs had detachable slatted wooden extensions that allowed you to sit with your feet elevated off the ground. One spring afternoon I had folded under the foot of one of these extensions and was using it as a slide. Suddenly I felt a sharp pain in my left buttock. I jumped up and felt my rear end. A huge splinter was sticking out through my underpants. I ran off saying, "I have to go!" over my shoulder. I didn't want Aunt Frances to see what I had done to her chair. In the protection of a nearby stone wall by the back door of the Palace I was able to pull up my dress and examine the damage without being detected. I grasped the four-inch-long splinter and tried to pull it out but it wouldn't budge. The pain was intense. There was nothing for it but to face the music and run home to Kitty. She got part of it out but a large chunk lay deeply wedged. We hurried across the street to the emergency room at St. Luke's Hospital. Finally, with what seemed like the entire medical staff of the hospital looking on with barely concealed amusement, the giant splinter was extracted. No one scolded me, no one was mean or unkind yet my feelings of shame and humiliation were as intense as the pain from the splinter had been.

During the last few years we lived at the Choir School; my father made it clear that he didn't want me going over to visit Aunt Frances all the time. He didn't tell me why, only that I was not to go there except when invited on special occasions. I felt both puzzled and deprived. Why couldn't I go see my best playmate? Sometimes I wandered in that direction anyway and when Aunt Frances would see me scuffing along the driveway she would wave and call for me to come join her. More than once, Daddy caught me talking with Aunt Frances when I shouldn't have and scolded me for disobeying. It was many years before I realized the reasons behind his restriction: Aunt Frances had a drinking problem.

Other Playmates

While I had several cousins I enjoyed playing with, two of them girls just my age, I only saw them from time to time. Mostly I had either Jay or Dudley as playmates or else I played alone. I rode my tricycle on the terrace in front of the school, swung on the swing and played "house" under the cascading branches of a great bush on the edge of the lawn near the driveway. Once I remember getting into trouble for making mud pies under that bush with my friend Ann. Ann was the younger daughter of the Choirmaster and she lived with her parents and older sister, Eunice, in an apartment across the street from the Close. She was three years older than me but we got on well, both enjoying dolls and other domestic activities such as making mud pies. Sometimes I was invited to Ann's apartment and we baked real cookies, under her mother's supervision. Ann, Eunice and I all went to the same girls' school, Saint Agatha's. In the mornings, my father and their mother took turns driving us and my brothers, who went to Trinity School a few blocks away.

On certain days the ice man arrived with his horse and wagon. When I saw him coming, I would run up the drive to greet him at the back door of the Bishop's Palace. First, I reached up as high as I could to touch the horse's unbelievable soft nose, gently lowered to meet my outstretched hand. Then the ice man would invite me to climb up on the wagon and sit next to him as he drove down the drive, around the corner to the back door of the school where he delivered ice to the kitchen. There I would dismount and wave goodbye, watching him descend the steep drive behind the school until he reached the street and disappeared in traffic.

In the winter when it snowed, I loved sledding with my brothers at the north end of the school where the ground sloped away gently. One winter, there was so much snow the choir boys made a huge snow jump there and went careening off it into space with their sleds. I considered that too risky and preferred digging out a snow house from the great pile below the terrace. When my cousin Sally came to visit, we retreated into our snow house to get away from all those noisy boys and shared secrets.

Christmas Cards

Every year in December, Jay, Dudley and I set out on an important mission that was both exciting and slightly dangerous. A few weeks before Christmas, my father set up a card table and chair in the living room of our apartment and there signed and addressed the envelopes for Christmas cards. These were colored reproductions of famous paintings of the nativity scene. Then we were summoned and given detailed instructions as to where the cards were to be delivered. Every person who lived and/or worked in the Close received a hand-delivered card. I was glad Jay was in charge because the instructions for how to reach some of the people were really complicated. Each clutching a handful of cards, off we went to remote corners to seek out people, some of whom we never saw except on this annual visit.

There was one aged couple who lived in a tiny apartment at the top of a long flight of narrow, creaky stairs. When we knocked on the door, it seemed to take forever before it was opened by a white-haired lady, all stooped over wearing a faded cotton print dress covered by a big apron. On her feet were black lace-up shoes with thick two-inch heels. She invited us in and offered candy wrapped in crackly cellophane, something unknown in our lives at home. Her husband sat in a chair, saying little. Unfamiliar smells assaulted my nose as I stood looking around at the cluttered space. Jay did most of the talking until it was time for us to go, at which point, we all three chimed, "Merry Christmas!" and departed hastily down the rickety stairs.

The maintenance men in the shop were easy to find. I went there often. I loved the smell of fresh sawn wood, there were always lots of interesting projects in the making, and the workmen were fun to talk to. The telephone operator behind her glass wall was another favorite. Her spot was at the bottom of the long rickety stairs. I used to stop by and talk to her and watch her operate the big switchboard with blinking lights and red cords plugged into different slots making a confused pattern of wires.

The ladies behind desks in the Bishop's office were always cheerful and friendly when we showed up with our Christmas cards. I wondered what it would be like to sit behind a big desk all day long and open stacks of mail. The head lady, the Bishop's secretary, was named Miss Gottschalk. Once I was old enough to understand the wonders of chalk and blackboard, I thought, "What a perfect name for the person who writes all the Bishop's letters for him!" Jay and Dudley and I would giggle about that as we'd make our way down the steps, turn right and head towards the Deanery.

Visiting old Mrs. Gates in the Deanery was never a brief affair. A semi-invalid, she sat in a big chair in her gloomy room pasting her used Christmas cards into huge albums. She was proud of her work and always invited me to look at the albums with her. She was especially appreciative of our pre-Christmas visit; it meant another entry into her collection. There was usually a plate of cookies on the table and I silently wondered if it would be greedy to take more than one when they were offered.

Quite the scariest of all the sorties was the one to the furnace room in the crypt of the Cathedral. To get there we had to descend a precariously steep flight of iron steps with no backs into an enormous dark space that seemed to have no walls or ceiling. There in the deep gloom were two giant furnaces giving off a deafening roar. As we stood at the bottom of the stairs blinking, trying to get used to the dark, out from the inky blackness emerged three inky black men. They towered over us, smiling broadly with a great show of white teeth. They were as gentle and soft-spoken as the scene was menacing and tumultuous. The furnace men took their cards and shook hands as though they had been handed a precious golden nugget. Sometimes one of the men would walk over to the furnace, open the door, revealing bright orange and yellow flames, and shovel in more coal. Then the roar would escalate sharply and dancing light from the fire would make eerie patterns on the walls.

I knew that the furnace men would not harm me in spite of their overwhelming size. What seemed frightening was the place itself; what power these men held in their hands as they stoked the mighty fires beneath God's house!

Sunday Lunch

Most Sundays we ate our midday meal in the school dining room. My father sat with his back to a window at the middle of the head table with the Choirmaster,

Mr. Coke-Jephcott, on his left. After my mother died, the place to Daddy's right was often taken by a visiting dignitary, family friend or other guest. We children sat directly across the table with our backs to the room. In the early years, our high chairs were brought down from upstairs but eventually even Dudley graduated to a grownup chair. There was a festive air to the meal, symbolized by oval glass dishes of celery, carrots, olives, and fancily cut radishes placed on the three long tables. I liked sucking the pimento out of the salty olives, (ripe olives I considered bland and less interesting). The celery I found tough and hard to chew unless I was lucky and could find the tender pale-yellow bits. The carrots were all right but the radishes were more exciting with their little petals and "stingy" white centers. The rest of the meal consisted of sliced roast beef or lamb, with gravy, mashed potatoes and a vegetable. Dessert was always a slice of vanilla, chocolate and strawberry ice cream with thin, crisp waffle-like chocolate filled cookies.

Once Bishop Manning came to Sunday lunch and, in his honor, the kitchen served fancy ice cream animal figures for dessert. Back in the days before home freezers, ice cream was a rare treat. People either made it themselves in a hand-turned churn on the back porch, brought it home from the ice cream parlor in little white cardboard containers and ate it at once or, as in this instance, had it delivered packed in mysteriously dangerous dry ice. ("If you touch it, it is *so cold* it will burn your fingers,"

I was warned the first time I saw dry ice.) The ordinary vanilla, chocolate and strawberry striped slabs were not good enough for this special event. So, the maids who waited table in the school served each person, starting with the guest of honor, a plate on which rested the form of a chocolate flavored rabbit, chicken, horse or other animal. I watched as Bishop Manning, for whom the word "dignified" was invented, take up his spoon. It came down innocently enough on the prone rabbit, too recently snatched from its frozen lair, made no dent there whatsoever, but bounced off the rock-hard ice cream and clattered noisily onto the plate. The rabbit shot diagonally along the shiny oak table like a well-aimed bowling ball and landed in the lap of one of the boys sitting three seats to my right. There was a moment of horrified silence. Then my father's booming laughter broke the spell, quickly followed by the Bishop's more moderate good humor. Very soon the entire dining room was buzzing with delight as word of what had happened at the head table spread throughout the room. We children talked about it with great glee for years. I think I felt comforted in the knowledge that if Bishop Manning, who stood very close to and only slightly below God, in my young estimation, could survive such an incident of public embarrassment and humiliation, perhaps there was hope for me.

Sometimes there were announcements to be made during meals. My father would pick up and ring a little bell that sat in the center of the table in front of him.

A change in the schedule, someone's birthday, a special meeting for prefects. One Sunday he brought the room to silence and announced, "I made a mistake at the eleven o'clock service this morning. Can anyone tell me what it was?" One boy thought he had sung a wrong note. Another suggested he might have mispronounced a certain word. My father dismissed these unlikely suggestions with good humor. Finally, a small boy at the far end of the room spoke up in an equally small voice, "Sir, didn't you, at the part where we sing the responses to the, the Ten Commandments, I think, sir, you may have sung the one about…the fifth one, before the one…, the fourth one, sir?"

"You're absolutely right, Dawson! Good for you for noticing." My father gave his famous "Ha!" laugh and beamed with pleasure; at least one of his charges had been paying attention that morning.

Occasionally we were invited to the Bishop's Palace for Sunday lunch. This meant extra care to see that hands and face were clean and hair brushed. As we walked out the door of our apartment to make the short journey across the lawn, Kitty, while admonishing us to behave, would hand Jay or me a small embroidered linen towel-like case neatly tied with a ribbon. When we reached the sally port door, we rang the bell and waited for it to be opened by a maid in a maroon silk uniform with white organdy collar, cuffs and cap. Solemnly we handed over the linen packet and went to the cloak rooms to leave our hats and coats. There was a spacious gentlemen's cloak room and next to it, equally large, the ladies' cloak room, each with their own lavatory. From there, we ran across the hall to the Ghost Room where Aunt Frances was waiting to greet us. After a time of exploring the toy cupboard and chatting with Aunt Frances, we would all make our way up the grand stone staircase to the second floor, turn left down a wide paneled hallway, lined with stiff chairs and fancy chests and dressers, to the great drawing room. There on a long brocade sofa sat the powdered Mrs. Manning, a vision of silk, lace, pearls, and perfume. To the left of the sofa, the diminutive Bishop sat bolt upright in an enormous brocade chair with carved wooden arms. My father was there as well and sometimes another guest or two. I would go first to Mrs. Manning and remembering to curtsy, shake hands and say, "Fine, thank you" to her, "Lovely to see you,

Jane dear. How are you today?" Being so close, I had a chance to inspect the amazing array of beads, chains, and jewels that hung from her neck and adorned her fingers. Next, I went to the gently smiling Bishop whose slender hand seemed overpowered by his huge gold ring with its etched purple stone.

The grownups were sipping sherry from tiny stemmed cut-crystal glasses. Mrs. Manning offered us each a cracker from the plate on the coffee table. These were not the kind we had at home, they were smaller, oval and tasted slightly sweet. Presently a maid appeared at the door to announce that luncheon was served. Everyone rose and filed back down the long hall to the dining room at the other end. My seat was always on the near side of a heavily carved mahogany table facing the huge stone fireplace, next to Aunt Frances, who sometimes cut up my meat. There was a cushion on my chair and a linen doily at my place. On each side of the doily lay the contents of the embroidered packet we had handed over half an hour earlier; my monogrammed little silver knife, fork, spoon and pusher.

For years my brothers and I used to taunt one another with the warning, "If you behave like *that,* you won't be invited back to the Bishop's house for lunch!"

Questions

As the years rolled by and I came to understand the meaning of those words spoken solemnly week after week by the important people in the Cathedral, I found I had a dilemma that seemed unsolvable. My mind formed questions I was unable to articulate. Some of the information I was receiving from the outside did not match up with what I knew on the inside. So, I kept my questions to myself and for the most part, tried to be a "good girl" and follow the rules.

Lurking in the shadows of my awareness was the possibility that my mother had left because of something I had done. It was *very* important, therefore, to do what I was told by my father so that he wouldn't suddenly disappear also and then I'd be alone, totally abandoned.

But even as I tried to follow the rules and doctrine laid out by my father, the questions continued to baffle me. Here is how I reasoned it out in my head. The important people inside the Cathedral agreed that there was an all-powerful God and that he controlled everything. They also agreed that God loves everyone on the entire earth – we are all God's children – and that we are supposed to love him back. If you wanted to learn the whole truth about how to love God and what to do not to make him angry, you had to listen to the important people and follow what they said you were supposed to do. What's more, those who didn't were somehow in trouble. There was an implication that anyone who didn't follow the directions laid down by the important people was going to be in trouble with God. This is where I ran into trouble myself. It didn't make sense to me that if God loved everyone, he could love those people *less* outside the iron gates of my world who clearly didn't know about what the Important People in the Cathedral were saying. When I walked with Kitty across the street to the grocery store, I saw lots of folks who I was sure had no idea what went on behind the great bronze doors. What about those folks? How come they were left out? Why would an all-powerful, all-loving God let that happen? It didn't make sense.

Then there was another problem. What about me? Where do I fit in? How come the men and boys get all the good parts? I knew I was not interested in flitting about on the fringes like the deaconesses but there was no role for me in my father's God-centered world. Here too, I had no answer to these troubling questions and it never occurred to me to ask anyone. Even if my mother had been there, I'm not sure I could have found the words to express my thoughts and feelings.

It wasn't until I came to study with the healer, Barbara Brennan in the early eighties that some of these questions received answers. In a private session with Barbara, I asked about my childhood at the cathedral.

She said, "[You had a past] lifetime where you were titled and at the end of that lifetime, you had grave questions about titles and values. So, in this lifetime you came into a situation again where those who are titled have very little to do with the value as you actually saw it and yet there was the ritual of empowerment through naming and titling. Thus, there is within [your] soul now the requirement to learn to balance value and to place titles upon that which is valued and see how the empowerment of a title will enhance the value and yet not change its innate value. That is to say, an entitlement enhances the visibility of an innate value. As a child in the Cathedral, you were fully as valuable as any other human being walking upon the floor and yet those with titles appeared as more valuable because their value was pointed out; was in a sense, carved out and honed by the power of the word." Barbara goes on to point out that titles are a way to point out and thereby enhance the spiritual power of certain individuals and traditions by enhancing their visibility.

At first, parts of this explanation seemed mysteriously dense and difficult for me to grasp and integrate. I was greatly relieved, however, by the notion of a past life in which I had come to question the value of titles as they relate to intrinsic value. Now I understood why I had been born into a situation fraught with titles—the Important People—where there was no possibility of my being one of the entitled. As I sat with this new information, I began to appreciate those early years in the Close from an expanded perspective. Rather than feeling left out and unimportant,

I have come to accept my early life situation from the powerful vantage point of co-creator.

Saddle Shoes

Everyone in the whole world wore saddle shoes except me. My cousins wore saddle shoes, my classmates in school wore saddle shoes, even my mother wore saddle shoes. But now she was dead and not able to see to it that I had *my* saddle shoes.

In the picture of my mother hanging above the head of my bed, she was wearing saddle shoes. She was astride a bicycle with my older brother Jay, aged about four, sitting in a basket seat fastened between the handlebars. They were in Bermuda. I had chosen that photo from a collection of many loose snap shots, large and small, some curled up at the edges that lay in an untidy pile in the top drawer of my mother's desk. Some weeks after she had died, my father called my two brothers and me together and told us we could each choose a picture of Mummy for our own and he would have it enlarged and framed for us. I was not yet five, Jay not yet seven and Dudley about two and a half at the time.

I was excited looking at all those pictures, some of them taken before I was born. I remember one of my mother that I particularly loved. She was perhaps sixteen, seated on a rope swing slung from the branches of a great tree, hair flying free, a wistful half smile on her face. The background was a bit fuzzy which gave the picture a romantic aura. I pointed to it and asked if I could have that one. My father seemed amused at my choice. He searched for the negative but, alas it was long gone. For some reason, the print in the desk drawer couldn't be released so I must choose again. I considered for some time and finally chose the saddle shoes picture.

The original snap shot was small but the negative was located and off it went to be enlarged. Later I remember going with my father to the framers to pick out a frame. I decided on a narrow hand-tooled squared wooden frame with a gold wash. These two decisions, the picture and then the frame, were the first time I can remember being invited to choose what I wanted for myself. When the picture was ready, my father brought it home and hung it on the wall at the head of my bed in the corner of the nursery which I shared with Dudley. That picture has stayed with me ever since and hung in my different bedrooms throughout the decades.

It must have been about three years after the picture choosing that the business of my having saddle shoes came up. I was in school by now and daily in the company of other girls, ranging in age from five to eighteen. Starting in First Grade we all wore uniforms to school: blue jumpers and white cotton blouses. I don't think there was a rule about shoes but almost everyone wore saddle shoes. Even at the age of seven or eight, I knew they were the "in" thing to wear. Every September my father took us to buy new school shoes but they were always sensible brown oxfords, never anything so frivolous as saddle shoes. The trouble with saddle shoes, he would say, was that they got dirty and scruffy looking very quickly and therefore were out of the question.

How I longed for a pair of saddle shoes, just like the ones I saw on my mother's feet in the picture over my bed every day! I became obsessed with acquiring this status symbol. I confided in Kitty. She was kind and understanding. She encouraged me to ask my father directly. Maybe, she suggested, if I asked very nicely, he would see how important it was to me and relent. So, one evening, with all the courage I could muster, I approached my father as he sat in our living room. Could I please have some saddle shoes this year? I was aware that being like everyone else was *not* a reason for doing anything in his book, so I wisely avoided that argument. Daddy wasn't angry at my request, nor was he persuaded by my great longing. He simply repeated, gently but firmly all the sensible reasons I had heard before. Saddle shoes got dirty and were unattractive, who would keep them clean? We were not rich enough to employ someone to polish my dirty saddle shoes daily. It was not important and I should put it out of my mind.

While he talked on, my mind's eye pictured Kitty polishing my brown school shoes and my white summer tennis shoes as I had seen her do time and time again.

If she could polish brown shoes and white shoes, why couldn't she polish brown and white shoes? I said nothing, however. Then I thought about the picture over my bed. Mummy wore saddle shoes, hers weren't scruffy and unattractive. She obviously thought saddle shoes were just fine. Still I said nothing. To try to talk about my mother with my father was unthinkable. Too scary. Too painful. I was up against a stone wall. I managed to cover up most of my feelings but inside I felt utterly powerless and devastated.

Though Kitty understood my need, she had no power in this situation, she worked for my father. My mother, who clearly approved of saddle shoes was no longer present. She had died and left me, I knew not why, to fend for myself. I went off to bed feeling totally alone with no one to turn to who could help me. It might have been easier if I could have been angry at a stern father but Daddy was affectionate, calling me "Jenny", his favorite name for me. He simply considered my request as a silly, childish notion that would pass. Of course, it was a childish notion! I was a child of eight. But it wasn't silly and it didn't pass.

Lanny Ross

Lanny Ross, a well-known tenor, popular in the late thirties and forties, had come back to the choir school where he had been a boy chorister. About twenty boys were gathered around him in the Common Room one evening, shyly asking questions and waiting impatiently for him to sing. In a carefully thought out conspiracy with Kitty, who was a great Lanny Ross fan, I slipped down the back stairs from our apartment on the second floor, crossed the hall past the open door to the Common Room, silently entered the darkened school dining room, and climbed up onto one of the great oak tables from which I had a splendid view of Lanny and his admirers through the partially closed sliding doors.

I felt excited by the thrill of participating in a daring adventure. After all, I had not been invited to this gathering; I was an eavesdropper and secret witness. At the same time, I felt invisible and therefore protected as I knelt on my heels in the dark; Kitty assured me no one would know I was there.

Lanny sang several songs in his honey-coated Irish voice, chatting easily with the boys in between each number. I could hardly believe this "famous person" was actually standing only a few feet away. In all of my eight years I had never been so close to a real live celebrity. I couldn't wait to tell my best friend, Betty, when I got to school the next day.

"Now, I want to dedicate this last song to the little girl in the blue dress with the pigtails watching from the dark. I don't think I've ever had such an adoring audience before." All eyes turned to peer through the three-foot opening in the oaken doors. I had been caught out! I battled with conflicting feelings: the thrill of being recognized and honored fought with the shame and embarrassment of discovery. In my confusion I blushed to the roots of my hair but held my ground, concealed my confusion behind a stoic smile and listened intently to "my song". Though I have long forgotten the melody, I can still hear the notes.

The Powder Puffs

In the First Grade at St. Agatha's School, our cubbies were square shaped, open-ended boxes. They were in two rows, low down along one wall under the windows of our classroom which overlooked West End Avenue. We kept our gym sneakers and other small items there. Above each cubby our name was printed neatly on a small piece of paper. Nowadays cubbies are much bigger, holding coats, hats, mittens, boots and lunch boxes. We had a separate coat room off our classroom and a hot lunch was served by the school. So, our cubbies were more modest in size but they were definitely considered our private space where we could store our treasures.

Sometime during the course of my First Grade year I had been given a small round compact with a mirror and a pale pink powder puff inside by a friend of my mother's as a play thing. This friend was fond of me and often gave me little-girl things. She was from the South and deliciously feminine as only Southern ladies can be. She had a laugh like the most delicate of wind chines, a mischievous smile and wore her black shiny hair in coiled braids above her ears. I thought she was exotic, glamorous and beautiful.

At first, I didn't know what to do with my compact, then I had an idea. I asked Mrs. Muncaster if she could get me some more little pale pink powder puffs just like the one in the compact. I needed about 12. I knew they were available because I had seen some at Woolworth's when I had been there with Kitty. Mrs. Muncaster wanted to know why I needed the powder puffs, so I told her I needed them for a project at school. My recollection is we discussed this on several occasions before I could convince her to buy them for me. I knew it was out of the question to ask my father to buy me 12 pale pink powder puffs and something told me Kitty might not be persuaded either, so I chose Mrs. Muncaster as my accomplice.

The word "accomplice" comes to mind rather than "helper" because there was an element of secrecy and illicitness to my plan. This guilty feeling I had that I was engaged in a questionable activity has stayed with me and puzzled me all my life. I never understood why I felt so uncomfortable until one day, about fifty years after the event, it suddenly dawned on me what it was all about, finally I understood. When I was six, however,

I only know my plan was important to carry out, no matter what the risk.

One day Mrs. Muncaster produced the little cellophane packet of the longed-for powder puffs. Off I went to school the next day with them secreted in my book bag. I asked my teacher, Miss Hillhouse, for a piece of drawing paper and a couple of thumb tacks. I explained that I was making a surprise for the whole class. I took the paper, tacks and powder puffs to my cubby and set to work. First the cubby was cleared of gym shoes and other items. Then I carefully arranged the powder puffs evenly spaced in the cubby with the open compact in the center. I remember struggling to be sure no one would see what I was doing. It was important to have it look just right, so I tried several configurations before I was satisfied. Finally, I dropped the tacked paper of the front of the cubby and went to ask Miss Hillhouse when I could share my surprise with the class. She promised to find a time during the day.

When the great moment came, I was uneasy, maybe even scared, but determined not to lose my nerve. Solemnly I walked to my cubby, knelt down and lifted the paper curtain. Then, one by one I called the names of the girls in my class to come over. To each I gave one of the powder puffs, Miss Hillhouse got one too.

I couldn't explain to anyone, least of all myself, why I felt compelled to perform this odd ritual, but perform it I did. All the time I had a vague knowledge that I was doing something forbidden. I think my classmates were a bit bewildered by my "surprise", what were they supposed to do with a small powder puff? I did feel, however, support coming from Miss Hillhouse and for all I know, she may have realized at the time what it took me fifty years to figure out. Once the powder puff distribution ceremony was over, my life returned to normal and nothing more was said of the incident.

Over the years, however, I have wondered about it; why did I do what I did? And why did I feel guilty about such a trifling gesture? As I asked myself these questions from time to time, I always ended up feeling slightly ashamed at having made a fool of myself. I couldn't get any farther than that.

Then one day, the incident came up in my mind yet again. Suddenly the picture was clear: the missing pieces fell into place. I was imitating the ritual of distributing wafers at Holy Communion that I had seen my father do countless times at the Cathedral. At six I couldn't understand too much about the meanings behind this rite but I had been going to church regularly since infancy and was well aware that it was *the most important* single act my father performed. What's more, I knew that handing out those little round wafers was a great honor and only certain special men were allowed to do it.

Now the First-Grade cubby business all made sense. After my mother died, I no longer had a female role model. My father was the only person in my immediate world I had left. The feeling of guilt and shame came from being conflicted between wanting to do what my father did and knowing that females weren't allowed to perform this most important rite. Growing up in the Close was a world where females had no central or important role. My father's professional life was tied up with being head of a boys' choir school and running the many events and services at the Cathedral. I was going to have to find *my* way of being special and giving something of value to others. My "surprise" with the powder puffs was my earliest attempt.

THREE

Precious Moments

Starting in the mid-fifties, I discovered that raising children provided many, many unexpected precious moments. Here is a tiny sample of the trunk-full of those memories that I cherish from my four children.

Honk

While our first-born was christened Henri, very soon thereafter he acquired the nick-name of Honk, which both family and friends happily picked up and use to this day.

One Spring afternoon in 1964, the school bus dropped off Honk (a third-grader) and Peggy (a second-grader) in front of our house in Bedford, New York (an hour north of New York City) from the little three-room school house they attended down the road.

As usual, I asked, "So, how was school today?"

Honk plunked himself down on a nearby chair and declared, "Mummy, the girls get their hands up *so fast!*"

I could see he was close to despair. Instantly my mind went back to my own childhood's unsuccessful struggle over my longing for saddle shoes. "This is important!" my inner voice recognized. Doing what I could to comfort Honk, I promised to talk to his father that evening when he got back from work in New York City.

Later, after the kids were in bed, I told Reg about Honk's urgent need for recognition at school. Both Reg and I were products of single-sex educations where we'd thrived and retained many happy memories. I remember suggesting that we look into sending Honk to the Harvey School, in the neighboring town of Katonah. Harvey was a boys' school, fourth through eighth grades. The following September, Honk went off to Harvey where he thrived academically, as well as socially. A happy camper.

During those years, we spent time each summer in Newport, RI with my father and step-mother. My father was a great sailor with a thirty-two-foot sloop, *Nautilus*. I noticed that when we took Honk sailing, he instantly fell in love with everything nautical: the boat itself, the rigging, being introduced to the challenge of sailing, the whole sea-faring world.

When he was in his last year at Harvey, the question arose – what next? I suggested we take a look at Tabor Academy, a boys' boarding school in Marion, MA, a coastal town on Buzzards Bay, just south of Cape Cod. After contacting the school and making an appointment, we drove up there one Saturday, talked to the Admissions Director, toured the school and then walked down to the harbor. There was *Tabor Boy*, a one hundred foot, two-masted schooner, one of Tabor's major "sports". Honk's excitement, while visibly contained, was nevertheless quite obvious. For the next four years, he excelled academically at Tabor, but his great passion was the time he spent aboard Tabor Boy, learning the ins and outs of nineteenth century seamanship.

When we arrived for Parents Weekend his first year, he was nowhere to be found around the school. So, we headed for the harbor. There he was, high up on one of *Tabor Boy's* masts, hanging over a square-rigged boom, happily furling a sail.

Honk (foreground) half-way to heaven

Peggy

When I called my father in Newport, RI from the hospital in Mt Kisco, NY to tell him I had given birth to a girl and that we were naming her after my mother: Marguerite Jay, he sounded pleased. Four hours later, there he was standing in the doorway of my room with a huge smile and holding an enormous bouquet of Marguerites (the blossom is a smaller version of the daisy). We were both so overwhelmed with feelings, we could hardly speak, so we just silently hugged one another.

Even as a new-born, Peggy bubbled over with energy, indicating an eagerness to get on with enjoying her life. She made friends easily and was greatly admired by her older brother, Honk.

When she was about four, she became fascinated by my sewing machine. She would come up to my bedroom, where the machine sat on an old enameled kitchen table in front of the window that looked to the west and the big field planted with sweet corn across the road. She loved to watch me sew, fascinated by the way the needle moved up and down seemingly all by itself, sewing two pieces of fabric together in a straight line or sometimes, by some mysterious trick, making a zig-zag pattern. She asked me how it worked and I showed her the floor pedal that I pushed with my foot to control the speed of the needle.

After watching for a while, Peggy asked if she could get down on the floor and help me by pushing the foot pedal with her hand. At first, I was hesitant, saying it was tricky to control and I didn't think she would be able to keep it from going too fast. "Please, Mummy, please, let me do it!" she pleaded, "I'll be *very* careful, I promise!" Clearly, she was determined to take on this exciting new challenge. I promised I would teach her to sew when she was older, but she was determined to participate *now*! I could see she had her heart set on being part of the sewing world, so we discussed how I could tell her when to press the pedal very gently at first and then, when I gave the word, to press it a bit more so the machine would go faster, but not too fast. It took a few practice runs, until she figured out just how much pressure to apply to the pedal. Before long, we had become a team, both delighted with our success at performing our separate and important roles.

Louise

Right from the beginning, I could tell that Louise was very different from her older sister, Peggy. She had a contemplative quality about her that seemed to be carefully studying the world around her as it came into view. One sunny Spring morning when she was about four, I watched her from the kitchen window, wandering around outside, exploring the wonders of new leaves on the trees, sprouts shooting up from the earth in the garden and the sights and sounds of newly returned birds overhead. She was happily chatting away to herself, thoroughly at peace with the world. Suddenly, I noticed her spot something on the lawn. She ran over and knelt down to examine this mystery more closely, her whole being consumed with awe and wonder, chatting all the while. Then she reached out and plucked this wonderous bit of life, stood up and came running into the house to show me her amazing discovery. "Look, Mummy! I found this *beautiful* flower, just growing there on the lawn!" Louise had encountered her first dandelion.

The summer before Louise went off to school, I decided it was important to prepare her for dealing with her birth date. "Weeze, you may not know, but some people think that Friday the thirteenth is bad luck. There's an old superstition that when the thirteenth of the month falls on a Friday, terrible things can happen. But *I* know that Friday the thirteenth is *very good* luck because that's the day you were born! So, in case anyone should ever try to tell you that you're unlucky because you were born on Friday, the thirteenth, don't believe them! For you and me, it was and is the luckiest day possible!" Louise listened thoughtfully to this new piece of information and then went off to play. Many years later when email entered all our lives, I noticed that she had chosen "louise13" as her electronic tag.

Paul

Seven years after his older brother Honk, Paul was born on St Patrick's Day. What, I wondered, would he bring with him that would further enliven our family? Lots, it turned out. The first summer Reg and I took all four children to Le Pin, the Gignoux family property in France, Paul was four. After the over-night flight across the Atlantic, we settled in, along with a couple of house guests, enjoying the beautiful long July days. That first evening, we were sitting in the garden anticipating one of the famous Anjou sunsets, when I realized it was already past Paul's bedtime. I called him over from exploring the nearby gold fish pond. "Do you think you could go up to your Tower room all by yourself, get on your jammies, bathrobe and slippers, brush your teeth and then come back here so I can read you a story before bedtime?" Paul thought that was a good deal, so off he went.

A little while later, the door to the front hall opened, and there was Paul. Thanks to my friend, Elsie, a talented photographer, that precious moment was captured for posterity.

At some point during those early years, we discovered that Paul was color-blind. The only color he could distinguish was yellow. Not wanting him to think of this as a handicap, I explained that color-blindness ran in my family. My mother's father, Grandpa, was color-blind and he had been a thoroughly "colorful", successful person whom we all adored. In addition, my older brother, Jay and our double-first cousin, Arthur, are both color-blind. They, in different ways, are certainly "colorful" and have accomplished much to be proud of in their lives.

Shortly after Paul started school, he developed an interesting ritual to help him deal with his color-blindness. In the morning, after I had woken all the kids, Paul's bedroom door, just off the kitchen, would open. He would emerge holding a shirt in one hand and a pair of pants in the other. Silently he'd came up to me and solemnly hold them out for my inspection. Most of the time I would nod and say, "OK." Occasionally I would suggest a different shirt. Paul didn't want to appear "weird" among his classmates.

FOUR

Reg's Ledges

One blustery Saturday morning in November of 1963, our friends, Buzz and Elsie showed up to help us embark on a project that Regie and I had been contemplating for some time. As I recall, it was Regie's idea: build a rope tow on the hill behind our house in Bedford for our four kids (and our friends' kids) to use for weekend skiing. Regie and Buzz set to work clearing away any trees in a line from the barn to the top of the hill. Their next task was to plant a series of posts along this path, each with a pulley near the top that would carry the circular rope back down the hill.

Meanwhile, Elsie and I had the challenge of creating a Long-Splice that would join the two ends of the five hundred feet of sturdy hemp rope that Regie had brought home from a Ship Chandlery in downtown New York City. Along with the rope, thankfully, came *Ashley's Book of Knots,* with illustrated instructions for how to execute a Long-Splice. First, Elsie and I brought the two ends of the rope into the house through the front door, having first made sure there were no knots in the outdoor portion of rope or that it wasn't wrapped around a tree. Because it was a chilly day, we wired the front door as closed as possible and draped a heavy winter coat or two over the part of the door still open to the weather.

With mugs of steamy hot tea in hand, we plunked ourselves down on the living room floor, in front of a roaring fire, contemplating the splicing instructions and the two rope ends.

1. Unwind strand A to point G; unwind strand B to point H; unwind strand C to point I.
2. Unwind strand D to point R; unwind strand E to point S; unwind strand F to point T.

This was the easy part. The third section involved carefully rewinding the individual strands of the two ends of the rope in order to make a circle. Then came the scary bit. It began,

3. *Cut* strand A at point J; *cut* strand D at point K; *cut* strand B at point L; *cut* strand E at point M; *cut* strand F at point N….

By the time we had completed our Long-Splice, we felt as though we had run a marathon—both spent from nervous anxiety and exhilarated from having successfully accomplished our assignment. When we took the splice outdoors to show Regie and Buzz, they were gratifyingly amazed to see the results of our efforts.

The source of power to carry the rope (along with eager young skiers) up the hill, came from our lawn mower, which was transformed into a ski tow motor. Every spring it would be restored to its original purpose, only to be reconverted again the following winter.

Once the circular rope was attached to the pulleys, all we had to do was eagerly await the season's first decent snowfall and then send out the word to our friends that Regie's Ledges was open for business.

That Christmas, our great friend, Bill Hoyt, presented us with a huge stack of cards that read:

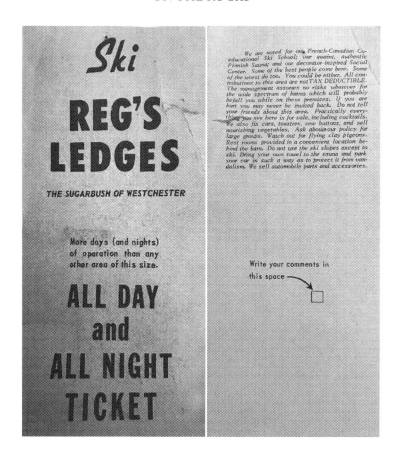

For a number of winters thereafter, on snowy weekends, Reg's Ledges was a popular gathering spot for our friends and their children to enjoy a day of short but nonetheless thrilling ski runs, after which we gathered in front of the living room fire for mugs of hot chocolate and homemade cookies.

FIVE

Following Directions

From early childhood throughout my life, moments (sometimes periods) of confusion pushed me to take action, with varying results. In addition, from time to time, without warning, I would find myself headed in a new direction without understanding why. Some of these directives were self-sourced, others came through— simply and clearly—what felt like, external non-material sources. What follows is a loose collection of stories and reflections that may seem disjointed. What they share is they all represent new interpretations of past experiences or "forks in the road."

Parenting

In 1956, a year after my marriage, I experienced an unexpected revelation when, one May afternoon, I took three-month-old Honk up the hill to the swing that overlooked our Bedford house and the large corn field across the road. As I held him in my arms and gently swung back and forth, this thought took shape in my mind: "Taking care of this child (and presumably more to come), will not only teach me how to be a loving mother, but at the same time I will experience what I had so sorely missed as a child: being lovingly mothered!" This thought signaled not so much a change in direction as a huge unexpected bonus!

For the next twenty years I enjoyed, not only raising my four children, but also, my life in Bedford. With my friend, Lorna, we created a business we called Can Do. In the community, we let it be known that we would take on all sorts of tasks that people needed help with such as driving people's cars from and to one of the three major airports that serve the NYC area (in those days, Bedford had no commercial airport service); organizing and running Tag Sales for people who were moving or just down-sizing and (with other partners) performing puppet shows for children's birthday parties. We became known as the "Can Do Ladies".

My Vision

In the midst of all these activities, in October of 1976, my husband, Regie, and I, along with Louise and Paul (the older two were away at college) and several friends flew to Le Pin, the property in the French Loire Valley that Regie's parents had purchased shortly after World War I. It consisted of a large fifteenth century chateau and gardens, plus two farms and vineyards. Regie was born, grew up and was home-schooled there, along with his four siblings. We were there to take part in the annual vendange (grape-harvesting).

Our first dinner at Le Pin was cheerful, even though we were weary from the long trip. Later that evening, I got into bed, turned out the light, and closed my eyes. Instantly I had a vivid image of myself lying in my own coffin, aware "they" were about to nail on the cover. What's more, I knew that once the coffin was sealed, no one would realize I was still alive! This alarming scene remained until eventually I fell asleep. The following night the coffin scene returned as soon as I closed my eyes. Every night for two weeks the same scenario repeated itself. As the days passed, the full meaning of this schema became all too clear. Meanwhile, I had three meals a day to prepare and host, our houseguests to entertain, as well as Louise and Paul to keep track of, checking to be sure they were keeping up with their school work assignments, and all with no hint of my alarming nightly visions.

The day after we returned to the States, I went into New York City to see my lawyer (an old skiing buddy of Regie's and mine). Thus began the most excruciatingly painful period of my life; the dissolution of my marriage. Without my ever-present memory of the Le Pin coffin image urging me on, I doubt I would have had the strength to persevere through the months-long ugly legal separation process (coupled with Regie's frigid hostility), while continuing to care for our children and carry on my other responsibilities.

As I was struggling to find my way through this nightmare transition, the memory of my fifth great grandfather, John Jay, kept arising in my mind. Somehow, I felt it was important for me to connect with his energy in order to help me find my way in my new life. Ever since I'd been very young, I had been exposed to stories of John Jay and his role in helping to create the United States. He and a handful of well-known colleagues, after extensive research and collaboration, came up with a plan that became the foundation for the United States of America.

While my personal difficulties were light years from the magnitude of tasks undertaken by my illustrious ancestor, I felt that if I could just connect to the energy of Jay's wisdom, it might help me sort out the tangle of obstacles surrounding me and point me in a healthy direction. Along with this strong intuition, I sensed that I needed to move back to New York City, the place of my birth.

A New Life

Finding a place to live in Manhattan was my first priority. Help came from an unexpected direction. A friend of my mother's told me that recently she had found an apartment by consulting a real estate broker. She gave me the name and number and suggested I give them a ring. In Manhattan, most real estate brokers don't take on rental properties; there's almost no profit in it for them. When I called the number I'd been given, however, and described the general location and size of the apartment I wanted, to my great surprise, the broker replied, "As a matter of fact, I do have something that might interest you." When I went to look at this three-room apartment, while it was by no means "a dream come true", I signed the lease that afternoon. For the next forty years, 201 West 89th Street, 7H was my home.

How come I was so lucky, I wondered? Here's what I ultimately discovered. In mid-July of 1978, the woman who lived in apartment 7H at 201 West 89th, died. The Super and his wife were planning to take their vacation for the upcoming month of August. He didn't want that apartment to remain vacant for over a month, so he persuaded a real estate broker he knew to take the listing as a favor. Clearly, his friend had a better chance of renting 7H in the two weeks before August 1st. It was at that moment that I stepped into the picture.

For the next few years, in an effort to make new friends, I connected with organizations I had known from the past: The Blue Hill Troupe, the NYC Smith Club and the Cathedral of St. John the Divine. After a time, it became clear that the first two of these groups were no longer where I belonged, even though the people involved there were open and welcoming.

Uptown at the Cathedral, however, I discovered the Dean, the Very Reverend James Parks Morton, was hosting a number of cutting-edge spiritual thinkers, teachers and practitioners. I found the Cathedral programs utterly fascinating. One day at the Close, while I was listening to the healer, Barbara Brennan speak, a voice in my head announced, "You need to learn what she has to teach you." While at the time, I had no interest in becoming a hands-on healer like Barbara, a few weeks later when she announced a series of classes, I signed up immediately. For the next two years, while studying with Barbara, I was exposed to masses of new information and new experiences! She helped heal my broken arm with her gentle touch. During another session, she channeled information that helped me sort out my confusion over why there was no role for me in my early life in the Close. She explained that in a past life, I had lived in a society where people's roles and titles were very important; they defined people's value. So, in this life, my job was to gradually create value from diligently interpreting the many different experiences of my own life. Studying with Barbara allowed me to access information intuitively rather than simply depending on the limitation of my rational mind.

The information I shared with Dr. Abrams and her young patient, James, at Harlem Hospital during my time there as a volunteer, is one example of tapping into that intuitive "knowing", as described in the next three stories.

A different venture into exploring Who Am I Really? put me in touch with Wind Eagle and Rainbow Hawk, a partially Native American couple who had created a practice—The Ehama Institute—that introduced people to the wisdom traditions of many of the indigenous peoples of both North and South America. They traveled throughout the USA, coming to the NYC area every few months, where twenty or so people spent the weekend at a retreat center outside the City, being exposed to the traditions and practices of the truly First Americans. One practice from the Cherokee people—Tslagi—especially attracted my attention. It consists of several rounds of a graceful pattern of circular movements using both arms and legs, repeated in the four directions. One thing Tslagi requires is balance: certainly, an essential element for surviving throughout an adventure-filled life. For over thirty years I've been practicing Tslagi first thing every morning.

Healing

It was during this period that I developed a series of workshops—Interpersonal Stress Management Systems (ISMS)—offering them in various communities around the country. I used to tell people, "We cannot change what happened, but we *can* change the story we tell ourselves and others about what happened." Gradually, this work shifted to a number of women independently contacting me, seeking help with their relationships with their mothers. After a time, some of them asked whether I would develop a weekend workshop so that they might delve more deeply into their mother/daughter issues. That July, I gathered with eight women at a retreat center in Maine for the weekend. The participants did good work and by Sunday afternoon, they left feeling considerably lighter. I, on the other hand, felt miserable, weighed down as though I had seriously overeaten. The director of the center, stopped by my room to say that she and a few friends would be attending a healing session that evening and wanted to know whether I'd like to join them. I jumped at this invitation.

About ten people sat on the floor in a circle. I can't remember the details of the first part of the evening but I do remember that I had my arms wrapped tightly around me, in an effort to contain my overflowing emotions. I couldn't speak. My distress must have been obvious, because the healer asked me whether I wanted to work on my issue. I nodded my head and when asked who I wanted to have as my helper, I pointed mutely to the retreat center director. Someone placed a large, sturdy pillow in the director's lap and I was told to move over and sit in front of her.

The healer then asked me if I knew the source of my pain. Without warning, I lifted my arms and began beating on the pillow in front of me. Along with these repeated physical assaults, I heard myself uttering guttural sounds of rage-filled pain. In the past, I had witnessed others experiencing similar moments of distress, but I never imagined *I* would be able to express such raw, primal feelings. Eventually, completely spent, I collapsed on the floor.

When I awoke the following morning, I saw the day was crystal clear and sunny, what I like to call "a Maine day". Moreover, the scene outside my window mirrored my feelings. No longer weighed down by my four-year-old pain, I felt feather light, open and free at last from my long-hidden feelings of rage. Once again, my life journey had unexpectedly taken me through a dark tunnel, only to deliver me into the glow of lightness and freedom.

White Water

A very different sort of adventure presented itself during the mid-eighties. One day, without warning, a thought formed itself in my head: What about taking up white-water paddling? My father was a great sailing enthusiast, so I had become familiar with that activity ever since I can remember. In the early eighties I had taken a trip through white water in the Grand Canyon. Along with a guide, we were eight people on a raft. While this was a thrilling adventure, I realized it was a very different experience from learning how to paddle a canoe or kayak down smaller rivers, through rapids.

My enthusiasm for taking up white-water paddling increased as I looked into where to find others who engaged in this sport. With a bit of research, I soon discovered The Appalachian Mountain Club had a New York/New Jersey White-Water Paddling Chapter with a Barn on the New Jersey side of the Hudson, not far north of the George Washington Bridge, where they stored a number of canoes and kayaks that members could rent.

For the next eight years, most spring, summer and fall weekends found me paddling down rivers with other white-water enthusiasts. The whole process was well organized: I was able to find other NYC paddlers with whom I could ride to and from my apartment and the Barn, as well as the Friday put-in and Sunday take-out spots. We camped out in tents and cooked our own meals. On the cooler weekends we wore wetsuits. As a beginner, I started out with a paddling partner, each of us kneeling in a position in the bow or stern of a canoe.

Before long, I graduated to paddling solo, kneeling in the middle of a canoe. Everyone wore a PFD (life jacket) because even experienced paddlers occasionally miscalculated the river and found themselves out of their boat in a flash. When this happened, the group assisted in rescuing both paddler(s) and boat(s). Year after year I looked forward to these lively weekend outings.

Then suddenly, I knew it was over. There were no disagreements or unfriendliness. I simply received a "message" that my time as a white-water paddler was complete. Some weeks after this occurred, I was sitting in my living room, thinking about all the great adventures I had experienced on those lively rivers. What had I learned, I asked myself, from my many white-water trips? The answer was right there: If you want to stay out of trouble, keep your attention on what's right in front of you, what's coming up in the middle distance and what's further down-stream, but still important, *all at the same time*!

IONS

Over the years, I have come to think of these activities as a prelude to my introduction to The Institute of Noetic Sciences (IONS). Founded in 1973 by astronaut, Edgar Mitchell, who, as he gazed out the window of Apollo 14 on his return from the Moon, experienced that *everything* (including all the millions of stars and planets throughout the universe), is *interconnected and interdependent*. Nothing in any of his extensive scientific training had suggested such a phenomenon. When he returned to Earth, therefore, Mitchell created IONS, designed to use the tools of science to study consciousness.

The headquarters for IONS is in Northern California. In the early years, three of their board members were New Yorkers. So fascinated were they by the discoveries being made by IONS' researchers and their colleagues, they were eager to have an IONS presence in New York City so that Easterners could be exposed to some of these cutting-edge discoveries.

In order for this to happen, the California IONS leadership decided that the East Coast enthusiasts needed to create their own official non-profit status. That accomplished, looking for someone to run this newly formed entity, they reached out to me to fill that post.

Thus, I became the President of Friends of the Institute of Noetic Sciences (FIONS). Over the next several years, FIONS invited leading scientists, spiritual practitioners and cutting-edge explorers from a number of disciplines to speak to us and help us begin to grasp ways to heal the long-standing science/spirit split. So many people were hungry to be part of this movement, throughout the USA and beyond, other local IONS groups sprung up until the IONS Community Group Network became an important supporting influence for helping IONS increase its reach. The IONS Community Group Network, along with supportive input from IONS, met a couple of times a year to share our different projects and to explore ways we might support one another to increase our members' awareness of life's interconnectedness.

Below is an excerpt from a document that one of my IONS Community Group colleagues, Shirley Freriks and I wrote in 2009.

> Today we see the results of that persistent curiosity. Much of the IONS-generated and supported research, theory, and practice has found its way into the everyday lives of millions of people around the world. Some of them may never have heard of IONS but they know the power of non-locality. Others may be practicing intention in their families, schools, work-places, communities without so naming it. Still others have learned to emulate natural systems by applying collaborative, rather than competitive strategies that recognize our essential interconnectedness and interdependence.

In addition to increasing our awareness of how science and spirit can act together in collaboration, rather than in competition, in 1998 and 1999, FIONS reached out to hundreds of the teenagers around the five boroughs of New York City when we created a program called: **Teens for Planet Earth**. The idea was to invite high school students to gather in groups of 2-5, find them a teacher from their school who would volunteer to help them get started and stay focused, as well as a FIONS member to act as Mentor to supply further support. We asked the students to consider the questions: "What kind of planet do we want to live on" and "How can we make our lives better?" Once they had agreed on a specific topic, their task was to create a poster visually expressing their idea. The motivating impetus was that the winning poster would be professionally printed with copies placed in the thousands of subway cars and busses of the NYC transit system for one month.

The first year, I was able to raise enough money to have one Teens for Planet Earth poster in the subways and busses. The second year, we raised more funds so that, not only could we have *four* winning posters displayed, but also, we published an impressive book—*Stop, think and dream*—designed, edited and published by FIONS members, Pat Kery and Gary Cosgrave, along with several other volunteer members with book-publishing skills. It displayed *all* the posters, photos of each team and described the ideas that led to their poster design. Every participating school Principal, student, teacher and Mentor received a copy of *Stop, think and dream*.

Twenty years later, I sometimes wonder whether those teenagers ever look back on that project and still value their expedience. As a Mentor for several teams myself, I definitely continue to cherish being part of Teens for Planet Earth.

Reviewing my years of being an active member of both IONS and FIONS, I realize all the people involved, starting with the founder, Edgar Mitchell, unexpectedly found themselves following directions that led them into uncharted territory. Maybe, I wondered, this is one way to describe evolution.

Released

Sitting in my living room one afternoon reading, I suddenly heard my father's voice saying, "You know, I'm not as thick-headed as I was when I was alive in a body." What!? These few simple words were both startling and revealing. Over and over I repeated them to myself, trying to grasp their full meaning.

Like most children, throughout my life I responded to my father's opinions or wishes by either inwardly accepting or resisting. In other words, I made choices, both large and small, either because of or in spite of my father's point of view. Now, without warning, I realized I had been released from that restriction. Because my mother had died when I was four, my father had been my sole authority figure throughout much of my life and, therefore, carried more weight than if I had been able to balance my choices between both parents. I jumped up out of my seat, bursting with energy. What Daddy was telling me was that his connection to me did not depend on his approval. We were simply connected by pure love: love that nothing and no one could drive asunder.

Unlike the other occasions in my life when I found myself spiritually directed in a new direction, with this brief message, I felt not only released from my father's influence, but at the same time, closer to him as a true comrade, free from judgement.

SIX

The Secret

In the early nineteen eighties, during my first years of volunteering with the HIV and AIDS pediatric patients at Harlem Hospital, I got to know and love a little boy, James. James had been born at the hospital and when I got there, had never been outside its walls. His mother had either died at birth or left him there, I'm not sure which. No family members were involved in his care. Such children were called "Border Babies." They actually didn't need to be in an acute care hospital but because of the widespread fear of AIDS, there were no other facilities—half-way houses, foster care homes—prepared to take them, they remained at Harlem Hospital. In those days there were no medicines or protocols for HIV

89

or AIDS patients and the very mention of those dreaded acronyms evoked enormous fear. The Harlem "Border Babies" were the subjects of intense medical research as doctors diligently searched for ways to arrest the growth of AIDS. James, who was almost three when I met him, was the darling of the seventeenth floor. Doctors, nurses, technicians, service staff and volunteers all enjoyed his mischievous sense of humor and loving personality. James shared a large room with several other "Border Babies" though he clearly was the star. When he was in a good mood, James loved to play little tricks—pretending he hadn't drunk his milk—when Dr. Abrams dropped by to see him at lunch time. He would gaze up at her with his huge, innocent-looking dark brown eyes framed by long curling lashes and a head of soft dark curls. When she discovered his milk was actually gone, they would both enjoy a good laugh together.

The Hospital's Volunteer Department procured three strollers, and with the permission from the physicians we started taking James and his comrades outdoors. A playground with swings and play equipment was just down the street and a bit further on was a small park with trees, grass, birds, squirrels. Witnessing the reactions of utter amazement from James and the other kids to these wondrous discoveries was deeply touching and rewarding. James would point to a squirrel running along the grass or scooting up a tree and then turn to one of us babbling excitedly with his enormous eyes full of questions, waiting for an explanation. Although it's a hard word to say correctly—squirrel—the kids were not shy in attempting it. Birds received similar attention. Some of the picture books upstairs in their room showed birds and various small squirrel-like creatures but we all recognize what a world of difference it is between looking at a drawing or photograph of an animal and encountering the living, breathing, food-gathering real McCoy just a few feet away.

About a year after the outdoor excursions started, we all noticed that James seemed to be regressing. He stopped talking, ate very little, didn't want to go outside and his bubbly energy was no longer available. One day when I was sitting with James reading him a story, Dr. Abrams came into the room. She and I had become friendly and she knew I was then studying with the energy healer, Barbara Brennan. She asked me, "Do you know what's wrong with him?" I was so taken aback by her question that all I could say was, "No!" When we were alone a bit later, she explained that she was concerned with James' regressed state. She especially wanted him to be in better shape at this time because in just over a week, she would be leaving to get married and would be away for ten days. She said that every time she went away, James' health tended to deteriorate. While I understood her concern, I could offer no insight.

Later that day, as I left the hospital and descended the subway stairs to go home, it came to me all at once and quite clearly—the full story—I did in fact know what was going on with James. A couple of days later, on my next trip to the hospital, I sought out Dr. Abrams but she was busy with a patient's family. "When you have a moment, may I have a word with you?" I asked.

When she came into the ward where James and the others were, I was once again reading to James. "You wanted to talk to me?"

"Yes," I told her, "I realized after I left here the other day, that I *do* have a possible answer to your question." I was on one side of James' bed and Dr. Abrams was on the other side. At this point James tried to push me away. He clearly didn't want me there. "I understand, James. This is hard to talk about but I think it's important that we do." James stopped trying to push me away but continued to look unhappy about my presence.

Facing Dr. Abrams across the bed, I continued, "This is what I know and this is the way that I know it. His entire life, James has been doing his best to please all his caregivers here. You, as his chief caregiver, the other doctors, nurses, people who come to take his blood, administer tests, bring him his meals. Everyone comes asking for something and he has always cheerfully complied." Glancing at James, I could see that he had calmed down and was sitting quietly in his bed, though looking somewhat dubious. "James is tired," I continued. "He's given all he can give and now he needs to go home, to truly rest."

Dr. Abrams seemed to be taking in my words and trying to fit them into her medical lexicon. As I remember, she said very little, nodding occasionally at my comments with a warm smile focused on James.

The following day, Dr. Abrams left to get married. I learned later that at the exact moment she and her husband stepped under the chuppah, James slipped into a coma and the following day his spirit left his body—he was on his way home.

After she returned to work, Dr. Abrams told me that following our conversation at James' bedside, she had put him in a wheel chair and taken him down to her office, "It was like the old days again. He was bubbling over, full of mischief, getting into all the rubber bands and paper clips and other stuff on my desk. We laughed and played just like we'd done in the past. He was his old self, full of life." As she spoke, I could sense her re-experiencing the precious final time the two had spent together, connected by pure love, with no emotional barriers separating them.

Her story made me remember times from my own childhood. When we were young, our father would announce unexpectedly, "Children, you're going to the dentist this afternoon. Go brush your teeth." We'd all pile into the subway and end up at a Broadway theatre to see such wonders as "Life with Father" or "Oklahoma!" Even though sometimes an adult would inadvertently spill the beans by saying something like, "I hear your father's taking you to the theatre next week," we kept the secret anyway because we didn't want to spoil Daddy's surprise. I remember these treats seemed all the more magical because everyone got to keep a secret. These secret-keeping adventures, of course, were motivated by love and gave us all great joy.

On the other hand, secrets that are based on fear can be life-draining and destructive. What happened after I gave Dr. Abrams my understanding of what was causing James' regressed condition, seemed to confirm that in James' mind and heart my interpretation was essentially the truth. Once his "secret" was revealed, he was released from what had been a heavy burden. Pleasing his caregivers—with Dr. Abrams as by far the most important caregiver—had been the central focus of James' short life. Obviously, his relationship to those who cared for him and came to love him had many of the elements of the classic mother/child relationship, that primary bond James had never had the opportunity to experience with his own mother. Perhaps the life-filled joy of James' final playful encounter with Dr. Abrams; their last time together, was possible because each had let go of expectations that were no longer viable and, causing them strain to maintain. They were able to find, therefore, complete pleasure in simply being together.

SEVEN

Marguerite

A couple of years after James left us, a beautiful little girl was born at Harlem Hospital and took up residence on the seventeenth floor. She was another HIV Border Baby with no family involvement. When I discovered her in a room by herself, she was no more than ten days old. I remember feeding her a bottle and marveling at her perfect tiny features and large questioning eyes. One of the nurses came into the room while I was there and we commented on her dainty, shy beauty. She told me that the staff had named her Marguerite. I always made a point of checking on her when I arrived at the hospital.

One day when I was sitting with Marguerite, holding her and singing her some of my favorite nursery rhymes,

Dr. Abrams came into the room,

"Oh, I see you've got our little baby with no personality." She said.

"I'm not so sure it's that she doesn't have any personality so much as the fact that she hasn't decided whether or not to stay," I replied. Dr. Abrams gave me a questioning look. "You know when sometimes you're going to a party or gathering of some kind and you arrive at the door, look around and realize you don't know a soul there. There's that moment when you feel torn between whether to step into the room, make the effort to find your host, introduce yourself to people and see what happens or there's the temptation to step back, turn on your heel and head home where you can unwind, settle down cozily by yourself with a good book and a comforting drink. I know *I've* had moments like that. It takes a lot of energy to show up and make your way in a whole new scene without a sponsor or buddy."

Dr. Abrams seemed to be considering my reading of the situation, but I got the feeling she wasn't convinced.

The next time I showed up at the hospital, she came up to me in the hall.

"Oh, I want to thank you for what you said last week!" she exclaimed.

"What did I say last week?" I wondered.

"What you said about Marguerite and her not having decided whether or not to stay," she replied.

Dr. Abrams explained that several days before she

and I had spoken the previous week, Marguerite's vital signs had started to go into crisis. A team of doctors and nurses worked on her and managed to stabilize her and bring her back. This is, of course, normal procedure in hospitals.

"Just a few days ago, her vital signs started to go into crisis again. I was summoned but as I stood looking down at our little Marguerite, I thought about your interpretation of what might be going on with her. So, I decided not to intervene. I let her go."

I could tell that this had been a difficult choice for Dr. Abrams, perhaps the first time she had ever made such a choice in her medical career. But what was clear was that her decision had been motivated by love not fear; thus, allowing her to erase what had been a heavy weight from her heart.

EIGHT

Coloring

You've got to be taught to hate and fear,
You've got to be taught from year to year.
It's got to be drummed in your dear little ear,
You've got to be carefully taught.
You've got to be taught to be afraid
Of people whose eyes are oddly made,
Of people whose skin is a different shade,
You've got to be carefully taught.
You've got to be taught before it's too late,
Before you are six or seven or eight,
To hate all the people your relatives hate,
You've got to be carefully taught.[1]

Is it really true, as the Oscar Hammerstein II lyrics from *South Pacific* say, that we "have to be taught to be afraid of people whose skin is a different shade"? For the first half of my life, my answer would have been yes. I would have agreed that prejudice is learned and handed down in families and cultures from one generation to another. That belief was challenged one day several years ago in a curious way. Quite unexpectedly I found myself participating in a little drama between a four-year-old and a young man that forced me to think more deeply about the roots of prejudice. It also helped me recall a puzzling incident from my own childhood that I had been unable to share because I thought it was shameful.

During the latter years that I volunteered at Harlem Hospital my assignment changed to the outpatient pediatric clinic. My role there was to help entertain the children while they waited to be seen by doctors and other medical professionals. Often families spent the entire morning at the clinic seeing more than one person. This can be hard on both child and parent alike. My tools consisted of a huge box of crayons, drawing paper, a selection of books, a memory bank of children's songs and games and my imagination. I loved being there; I got to play. Every week was different and I never knew who would be there or what might happen. Consequently, I learned to take my cues from the children and try to respond to their needs of the moment.

One morning there were about half a dozen young children in the waiting room when I arrived and a new volunteer, David, had already brought out the drawing and reading materials. It was a happy scene at the round table with several artists between the ages of two and five seated in little chairs busily creating masterpieces. Parents, foster parents and grandparents were seated around the outside of the room, some holding tiny infants. I said a general good morning to everyone and joined the group in the center.

After a few minutes, Jessica, aged four, came rushing up to me in great excitement.

"Tell him to go wash his arm!" she cried, pointing at David with a look of mixed defiance and suspicion. In the months I had known her, I had come to love Jessica. She was a bundle of energy, fiercely independent and utterly charming. What now, I wondered? Jessica tugged at my arm, insisting, "I don't like his arm, it's dirty. Tell him to go wash it!" I could see she was really upset.

I looked at David's arm. David has a birthmark that covers most of his left arm and part of the hand. Oh, boy, I thought, here we go. I looked into David's eyes. His expression told me I had his permission to tackle this one head on.

"Oh, Jessica," I said, putting one arm around her waist and taking her hand in mine. "There's nothing wrong with David's arm, that's just the way he came."

"Well, I don't like it!" insisted Jessica. "It's bad and

ugly and I wish he'd go away!"

I reached over and gently touched David's arm. "Is this what upsets you?" I asked. Jessica nodded, frowning. "Well, let's think about that for a minute. Let's take a look at *our* arms." I said, placing my pale arm alongside Jessica's little brown arm. We both stared at our arms, saying nothing. "Your arm is a different color from mine, right?" Jessica nodded in agreement. "Do you think either of us has the wrong color arm?" She shook her head. "How would you feel if I said your arm was the wrong color? Or what if you told me my arm was not right?" Jessica didn't say anything but I could see she was busy thinking. "I might feel sad if you told me my arm was bad and ugly." I said. We were two buddies, shoulder to shoulder trying to work through a knotty problem.

"But I'm *afraid* of his arm, it scares me," Jessica finally blurted out.

"Ah!" I said, sensing a way out of this dilemma. "You know what you could do, Jessica? You could go over to David and just touch his arm and make friends with it. I'm sure he won't mind. It's very true that it's different from yours or mine but it's a good arm. It won't hurt you." I could tell from Jessica's expression that she wasn't convinced, but she was no longer upset so I let the matter drop and we both went back to coloring.

Twenty minutes later, there was Jessica again, tugging at my arm. "I did it! I touched his arm!'

"Great!" I grinned. "What happened?"

"Nothing, it was OK!" Jessica fairly glowed with success. We both stood there, thoroughly pleased with ourselves.

Ever since that morning, I have been mulling over what happened. It seemed clear to me that Jessica's fear and apprehension when she encountered David's birthmark did not stem from learned prejudice. I concluded she was simply frightened by something new and different. Her brain told her: skin doesn't come in that color. Beware! Danger! Because of her outgoing, uninhibited nature, she was able to tell me about it.

I thought back to my own childhood. How had I reacted to people with different colored skin"? Suddenly, I remembered a scene on the back porch of a summer house we shared with friends when I was about seven years old. I remember watching Tony, the black man who worked there, talking with my younger brother, Dudley. He reached out and took Dudley's arms in his great gentle brown hands. Fascinated, I stared, wondering whether the brown would come off on Dudley's skin. I was sure it would. Just like the nasty-smelling brown medicine that I had been given by the doctor for my eczema came off on my clothing.

To my astonishment, Dudley's arms showed no sign of brown when Tony released his hands, stood up and walked off in the direction of the barn.

Unlike Jessica, I had never told anyone about my

concern. In time, I became ashamed of being so ignorant as to think that brown skin was the same as brown ointment. Jessica helped me to understand my childhood confusion and to release the shame. What's more, she taught me how important it is to name the fear, to share it with others and go right up and touch it.

While it's true, we are often "taught to hate and fear", It is also true that we can be taught to love and trust. It seems to me that an instinctive fear response, which can develop into prejudice when people encounter something different from what they know; be it about race, religion, behavior or lifestyle, actually stems from insufficient information; a kind of innocent ignorance.

Jessica had no information to help her understand David's birthmark, so she made a faulty decision. In the same way I had made a false assumption as a child. After the Coloring incident, I determined to be more like Jessica: turn to those who can teach me when I'm confused and then, armed with more facts, reach out and confront my fears.

NINE

The Tea Set

On September 7th, 1984 my older daughter, Peggy gave birth to my first grandchild. When her husband, Dennis, called me from the hospital about 9:30 in the morning, to tell me the news, I was in a state of rapidly escalating, though still contained, anxiety. I had been alone in their apartment in Brookline, Massachusetts, with no updates on progress since the previous afternoon.

My pattern in situations of this kind is to occupy myself with physical activities. I guess this helps to release pent up energy as well as giving me the illusion of accomplishing something useful. On this occasion, I remember scrubbing everything in sight: the kitchen stove, sink, fridge, walls, cupboards. Then I moved into the other rooms and kept myself busy polishing and scrubbing there. When I couldn't find anything more to clean, I ironed everything I could get my hands on and still there was no word from the hospital.

Every time my mind began to develop possible scenarios, I forced it to concentrate on the task at hand rather than fantasies of what might or might not be happening a few miles away. I knew that if I allowed myself to dwell too long on what might be, my feelings would be out of control in no time. The housework helped to keep me from losing it completely. Of course, I stayed off the phone in order to have the line open for "the call", so support from friends was out of the question. Toughing it out alone is another familiar pattern in my life. Finally, I went to bed expecting to be awakened during the night by the ring of the telephone but when I awoke in the morning there was still no word. So, I went back to scrubbing.

When the phone finally did ring, Dennis' voice announced they had a baby and that Peggy was OK. Before he would tell me whether it was a boy or girl, however, he wanted to know what my "psychic" had predicted.

Earlier in the year, I had been to see a female psychic

and she had said she thought the child was a girl. I had told Peggy and Dennis about the prediction but did not reveal the content. So, when Dennis asked, "What did your psychic say?" I replied, "She said, 'It's a girl.'"

"Well, she was right," was his next remark.

All during the pregnancy I had heard no word as to possible names for this child and had not inquired. Even now, over the phone, Dennis did not give me any name for his first born. I remember thinking that was odd, but my role was to be supportive, not controlling so I said nothing other than expressing my relief, joy and delight at the happy news. Dennis related a few of the details of a long and difficult labor ending in a Caesarian section completed just minutes before. When I hung up the phone, I was bursting with energy which sent me into another whirlwind of activity. I probably started calling people, though I don't honestly remember. What I do remember is a new kind of anxiety began to build, or more accurately, began to surface from my subconscious where it had been quietly smoldering. I wasn't too sure what it was all about but somehow it had to do with the name for this new little girl.

In due course Dennis appeared, exhausted but elated and we returned to the hospital together to see mother and child. Holding my peace as long as I could, finally, I blurted out in the car, "What have you decided to call your new daughter"

"I'd rather wait and have Pegs tell you that herself,"

was his reply. This continuing mystery was feeding my anxiety like dry twigs to a bonfire. Eventually we found our way to the correct floor where I caught my first glimpse of this brand-new person in her little Plexiglas crib. She was gazing around in wonder and with great interest in her new surroundings, much like the tourists on Fifth Avenue in front of Rockefeller Center. Her mother was still in recovery and hadn't made it up to her room. When she did appear on a stretcher, I remember being shocked at how puffy and swollen she looked. It was obvious her little body had been through a lot. Her great joy, however, transcended any physical discomfort as she greeted us in the hall. "Isn't she great?" she cried from her rolling palate. "And Mom, we've decided to call her Emily Jane!"

It was as though an enormous block of ice had unexpectedly seized and encased my heart. Unprepared for this sudden internal climate change, I had no idea what had triggered it. Knowing I needed to say something supportive, I asked, "What will you call her?

"Oh, I don't know, Emmy most likely."

The block of ice doubled in size. "That's wonderful, darling! I'm so happy for you!" I managed to continue to mouth the appropriate words all the time wondering if they sounded as phony to Pegs and Dennis as they did to me.

Somehow, with an enormous effort, I managed to isolate the person inside me who was frozen and put her on hold, rather like a patient waiting in a doctor's outer office. The ice problem, I realized, would simply have to wait until I could give it my undivided attention. Clearly now was a time to give my unconditional love and support to this wonderful new family. As I perched on the window sill of Peggy's hospital room on that sunny September morning, I remember feeling so fortunate to be attached to these three people who were happily absorbed in getting to know one another.

Perhaps it was the next day or even several days later that I found myself alone and able to address the person with the block of ice around her heart. What was this all about, I questioned? It appeared I was upset that this little girl had not been named after me. Why was that so important? Was my ego really that out of control? Why did it matter what her name was? After all, her second name was Jane, wasn't that good enough? Clearly it wasn't, given the block of ice. It seemed as though I wanted to control the naming of this child. Why? At first, as I probed into this mystery, I was tempted to make myself wrong for my intense reaction and tried to talk myself out of it. The more I took this tack, however, the more the block of ice remained in place. None of my attempts to remove it had any effect. There it stayed, less intense to be sure, but frozen in place nonetheless.

One day, a couple of weeks after I had returned home from being with Peggy and helping her as housekeeper-nanny-granny, I was once more trying to understand the meaning of my icy heart. All of once a scene unfolded:

An eight year old, I'm standing in front of a drop-leaf table at one end of the dining room of our apartment at the Choir School in New York City, gazing at a very large, and to my young eyes, very ugly tea set. It is mine, I have been told by my father. This information has been conveyed with the clear implication that I'm receiving something of extraordinary value. While I've seen it many times before in my maternal grandparents' house on East 73rd Street but have paid no attention to it. Now, here it is before me, where I can study it at my leisure. My grandmother has recently died and the tea set would have gone to my mother but she herself died four years earlier. So now this formidable heirloom is mine.

I stand there trying to come to terms with this new responsibility. Why did it have to be so large, ornate and ugly, I wonder? Why couldn't it be simple and beautiful like my mother's silver tea set that I'm used to seeing? How am I ever going to make friends with this great monstrous thing? My father has explained to me that it's very special and has been handed down from mother to daughter for several generations. The name of the original owner, Jane Anthony, is engraved on the teapot, creamer, and sugar bowl. Hanging above the tea set on the wall is her portrait, set in a massive gilt frame, in poor condition. As I gaze at this lady, I can't help thinking that she was even uglier than her tea set! In addition to Jane Anthony's name, the teapot has inscribed on it the names of the other previous owners, including my grandmother. Directly below her name is mine, Jane Hughes, newly engraved.

My attention focuses on that list of names. This is how it looks:

Jane Anthony
Margaretta R Anthony
Jane Kip Anthony
Marguerite Montgomery Soleliac
Jane Hughes

As I study the list, one thing becomes apparent. The generations alternate between Jane and Marguerite. What if my mother had not died and had been alive to inherit this tea set? Why the pattern would have been broken! My mother's maiden name was Marguerite Montgomery Jay. So *that's* what went wrong! They gave her the *wrong name*! That's why she died, my eight-year-old mind reasons. I have finally figured it out. I knew there had to be a reason; things just don't happen for no reason. For four years I have been trying to understand why my mother had died and left me. Now I knew; it wasn't her fault at all, she had been given the *wrong name*! If she had lived, the pattern on the tea pot would have been ruined.

At this moment of discovery, I swore to myself that if I ever have a daughter of my own, I won't make such a grievous mistake. I will give my daughter the proper name, Marguerite, so she can grow up and live a long and happy life and inherit the tea set from me.

Twenty years later I was able to fulfill that promise when I gave birth to a daughter and named her Marguerite Jay. As this scene of long ago played itself out in my mind's eye, I finally understood about the icy heart. It belonged to that little girl standing in front of the tea set.

She was terrified that her precious little granddaughter had been given the wrong name! And she dared not let herself think about what that might mean so she froze her heart in ice to keep away the scary feelings.

It's taken some time and persistent patience to convince that eight year old girl it's really OK about the name. But now, she's so happy not to be carrying that secret terror anymore and the tea set is just a few pieces of finely worked silver, no longer an all-powerful, controlling presence. And most important, she _loves_ spending time with Emily Jane, who, we both agree, has exactly the right name.

TEN

Miles and Granny Take a Walk

One summer day in 1991, I learned something about relationships from my five-year old grandson. In the sweetest, gentlest way imaginable I was shown how I could enter a world of new possibilities by merely shifting roles. The beauty of the lesson, with all its ramifications, continues to amaze me.

Peggy, Dennis their two children and I were spending a few days with my step-mother, at her house in Newport, Rhode Island. On Sunday afternoon, my grandson, Miles, aged five, and I were given the task of returning a movie to the video store. We set off on foot for the shopping center, about a half a mile from the house. My plan was to stop at the ice cream store after we had dropped off the movie, though I didn't tell that to Miles in advance, thinking it would be more fun to surprise him. To get to the shopping center, we zigzagged along some quiet back streets, chatting happily as we went, cut through an empty parking lot and emerged onto one of the main streets of the town. From there we continued along the brick sidewalk until we came to a major street intersection with lights, complete with left-turn arrows, and WALK signals. At this point I took Miles by the hand and told him we would have to hurry to get across before the WALK signal changed. I knew I would feel safer if I had Miles by the hand. The fact was, I didn't trust him to stay with me and be aware of the lights and cars turning left and right on all sides. That was too much to expect from a five-year old. He took my hand without a fuss but I noticed, as we scurried across the street, I was having to pull him along. In spite of my urgings, he wasn't keeping up, but dragging his feet. We made it safety to the other side, nevertheless, and walked along the sidewalk looking in at the shop windows. Keeping hold of his hand, I noticed he continued, ever so slightly, to hold back, resisting my pace. When we reached the shopping center where the video store was, I let go of his hand but cautioned him to look out for cars. He headed straight for the video store, looking neither left nor right. A couple of times, when I spotted a car headed our way, I took his hand again, to avoid potential danger. He seemed cheerfully unaware of any hazards.

Eventually we reached the video store, returned the movie, and then went next door for ice cream cones. Miles is good company; we both were enjoying the outing. The trip back was much the same as before. Whenever I took hold of Miles' hand, by now sticky from the ice cream, I felt him resisting me, a persistent tug on my arm. Instead of taking the same streets, however, I decided to pay a quick visit to the art museum, which was on our way by a slightly different route

The museum is set back from the street on a spacious lawn with large trees. When we emerged from looking at some paintings of nineteenth-century ships, I suddenly had an inspiration. It wasn't so much that I had an idea and then decided to act on it. It was more that I found myself doing something before I realized what I was up to.

Here's what happened: I said, "Miles, why don't you be the leader and I'll close my eyes and you can take us back to Great-granny's house?" He didn't have a chance to decline because I already had my eyes closed. He accepted the challenge at once however, grabbed my hand, and began to lead me across the lawn. Now I was the one resisting his lead. Even though both of us knew the way, without my eyes I was cautious. I didn't want to stumble or run into anything. Would Miles know what to do when we reached the sidewalk? Would he be able to cross the side street safely? Would he look both ways for cars? Would he warn me when we came to the curb? All these questions were racing through my head as I allowed him to guide me from the lawn into the museum parking lot, and from there onto the sidewalk. I could feel both his little hands holding my right hand securely, pulling me forward. Now that our roles were reversed and he was in charge of getting us home safely, he knew exactly what to do.

I must confess, I did peek a few times, just to be sure we weren't going to run into any cars. After all, he was my responsibility and it was unthinkable that anything should go wrong.

He caught me peeking once and said "Now Granny, you're not supposed to open your eyes!" I promised not to do it again but made him promise to tell me when we got to the curb so I wouldn't trip and fall.

He didn't exactly tell me we had reached the curb and were about to cross the street but, like a seeing-eye dog, he stopped. I opened one eye a tiny sliver and could just make out Miles, staring intently at the curb, as though practicing thought transference. The same thing happened when we reached the curb on the other side of the street. He stopped and waited for me to figure out what to do next.

For the last part of the journey, we had to walk along a one-person-wide sidewalk for half a block, turn left, cross another side-street and then it was only a few steps to Great-granny's driveway. Miles picked up the pace as we went. I felt as though we were flying.

When I complained, he said, "Don't worry Granny, this is how we have to go to get home." Clearly, he was enjoying his new role.

Then, crunch, crunch, I felt the crushed stone of the driveway under my feet. I opened my eyes. There was Great-granny watering her garden and there was Miles looking so pleased with himself! Our little adventure had been a big step for both of us.

ELEVEN

Journey to Nevada

Two white converted school busses pulled up in front of the community center in the tiny desert town of Beatty, Nevada. We were led, handcuffed, into a large, empty room and told to wait. It was then I saw Louie, still wearing his brown Franciscan habit. He came in through the door smiling easily and almost at once spotted a young man he apparently knew. Without hesitation he walked over to the young man and in one huge sweeping gesture lifted his arms, bound at the wrists, up and over the fellow's head, then down his back-side, holding him in a warm embrace. It was such an easy, natural gesture, accompanied by words of welcome and comfort. "Wow!"

I thought to myself, "That's how I want to be: light-hearted, loving, compassionate." It was true, of course, Louie had been arrested many times over the years. Nevertheless, as I contrasted his performance with mine, I was aware of how much I had to learn about letting go and surrendering. When I saw how Louie radiated faith, hope and love from the center of his being, I resolved to keep at it until I could do the same.

Presently one of the marshals came and cut away our plastic handcuffs. Then I saw Louie in a corner of the room, remove his brown robe, fold it reverently and with this gesture return to his chosen disguise as an ordinary man. In his plain black tee shirt, cotton trousers and sandals he could have been a truck driver, a salesman, a farmer, anyone at all. In fact, Louis Vitale is no ordinary man. He is the head of the Western Provence of the Franciscan Friars, with extensive responsibilities and very much the spirit behind the protest and vigil movement at the Nevada nuclear test site. Except for brief moments, he prefers to remain in the background, allowing others to coordinate the many complicated preparations that go into these protests. How exhilarating to be in the presence of a person who had no need to prove his power by attempting to control others. Here was someone who understood the source of his power and who obviously knew that no one could rob him of it. That, combined with his utter honesty and compassion marked Louie as an example of a true leader. If such people were prominent in government and business, I mused, how different a world it would be!

So many impressions and insights had been piling in on me during the past few days. I didn't know how to make sense of it all. I felt battered and torn asunder as recent events picked me up, caught me off balance, turned me around, then pulled me forward at dizzying speed, forcing me to look ever more deeply into, "Who am I?" and "What is the meaning of all this?" I thought I had come here to be a Peace Maker. Now, through Louie's example I saw I had much to learn before I could claim that title. I was beginning to realize this was a personal journey of surrender. Surrender in the sense of allowing, letting go of having to control, ceasing to resist. Only then would I be able to enter the world of non-violence.

* * * * * * * * * * *

In April of 1987 I went, along with nine other women from New York City, to Nevada to participate in a civil disobedience action at the nuclear test site in the desert, 65 miles northwest of Las Vegas. When I made the decision to go, I had no idea what lay ahead. It was as though an internal force was urging me to take my ideas and methods for resolving personal conflict, (Making Peace) into a larger arena and put them to a new kind of test.

At the time, I taught interpersonal communication skills in order to help people live more balanced lives through understanding their internal experience and connecting it to their external relationships. Here was an opportunity to practice what I preach on a broader scale. What influenced me to go?

Certainly, a key factor in this internal nudging process had been the PBS series, EYES ON THE PRIZE. Aired in New York during the preceding January and February, it is the retelling of the Civil Rights Movement in the South during the 50s and early 60s, through newsreels of the period, a dignified narration and current commentary by a number of participants. As I watched it week after week, I was profoundly moved. Here were people, many of them still children who had been willing to put their lives on the line for what they believed. What was *I* doing?

In addition, as I read accounts of others who had participated in nonviolent protests in Nevada and elsewhere, I would ask myself, "Is this for me to do?" Finally, one day, as I finished reading a newsletter describing the February, '87 action at the test site, I heard myself saying out loud, "Yes!"

The Friday before we left for Nevada, the Ecumenical Coalition for Peace and Justice held a commissioning service for the people from New York who were going to be part of the Good Friday witness in the desert. It was in the course of this service that the reality of what it means to become part of a powerful movement dawned on me. I shifted from a "head" knowing of this commitment to a blood and bones knowing. There's a big difference, I discovered.

About twenty-five people gathered outside the Riverside Research Institute on West 42nd Street. The Riverside Research Institute is a Pentagon think tank engaged in nuclear weapons research. We handed out leaflets describing the hazards of nuclear testing to passersby. After an hour or so we moved into the lobby of the building and arranged ourselves into an oval against one wall. The Reverend Ralph Thompson, a Presbyterian pastor, who, up until that moment I had experienced as a gentle, patient, amiable soul, opened the ceremonies by stating our purpose in a booming, powerful voice. As though speaking from a mountaintop, he let it be known that this was a religious service of worship held outside the Riverside Research Institute, (decibels up) to commission certain persons to go on a mission to Nevada to protest the testing of nuclear weapons.

I had been brought up in a family of preachers and my father was nothing if not outspoken, but, this public display propelled me into an involvement with the world that I had not anticipated. My body became a pillar of stony aloofness clothed only in embarrassment. There we were, a little band of rag tag people, in a public place with strangers hurrying to and fro intent on their business. I felt their eyes piercing me with skepticism, indifference and distain.

"How tacky!" My stone-cold aloof self muttered. "I want no part of this. Why does Ralph have to speak so loudly? What if some of the people I *know* in the building come by and see me?" My private decision to make a stand for Peace and Justice had suddenly taken a most unexpected and alarming turn! So, this is what it means to be a witness of faith. You have to actually do it out loud in public! My resistance to being there was enormous.

Led by a guitar, we then sang several verses of "Down by the Riverside" "I'm goin' a lay down my sword and shield down by the riverside ... I ain't a goin' a study war no more." I had been singing that song with friends at summer picnics under the stars since childhood and had often thought about its meaning. Now it took on a new dimension and immediacy. Part of me was struggling to disengage myself from this scene, while another part, tentative and fragile, was experiencing something quite different. As I stood there, a reluctant player in a carefully staged drama, cracks appeared in my stony pillar of aloofness. Deep feelings were welling up inside me, feelings of release and then relief.

The service continued. Each person going to Nevada stepped forward in turn to receive an enameled dove of peace from the artist who had made the beautiful pendants and which we then wore around our necks as a symbol of our commitment to Peace and Justice. As this was happening, we recited the commissioning words together.

"(Jane), go in God's Peace."

Now the last vestiges of stony aloofness vanished and my heart filled with joy, and longing. I accepted my place in this new family. This was but one in a long series of acts of surrender.

A few days later in Nevada, I found myself going through similar barriers. Again, and again, as had been the case in our commissioning service, I was affected by the carefully planned and skillfully executed process. The staff and volunteers of the Nevada Desert Experience, (NDE) constantly invited us to come to our own conclusions or decisions. Options and possibilities were presented but it was up to us to figure out the how, when, where and why of our participation.

A good example of how this philosophy was played out occurred during the day of training before the Good Friday action in the desert. A hundred people had gathered in a community hall on the outskirts of Las Vegas for a whole day of non-violence training and preparation. One item on the agenda was THE HISTORY OF NON-VIOLENCE AND CIVIL DISOBEDIENCE. Instead of the usual talk one might have expected, a young man stood up and in a few short minutes related how he had come to be active in the movement, how people and events, public and private, had influenced his life. He invited us to do the same in groups of eight.

In our group, we spoke of private memories throughout our lives that had contributed to our being present. Since we had no time to prepare, we simply shared whatever came to mind. Then a designated person from each group summarized what had been said for all to hear. Ours was the last group to report and our reporter, Nancy, read from notes she had taken.

"How did I end up on my path? I've always felt there was a purpose in my life ... My Mom, persecuted throughout her life ... I was brought up nonviolently ... BEYOND WAR, the basic premise being: *war is obsolete* ... My two sons I brought up non-violently, no guns ... My family listened to Mozart ... My father was gentle and lived a simple life, he really believed in Christ, to do the best he could in life and for his family ... Priests and nuns, live your values was a strong message through them ... my younger brother, Ray, his innocence has so much to teach me ... Since I was little, I had an abhorrence of violence ... My father, was violent in many ways ... The way I went through the appallingly violent experience of my marriage separation: It taught me a lot. There's Quaker in my background ... My parents were simple-living people, no credit cards. After an initial, resentment, I came to appreciate that ... Mother Teresa, I was drawn to her bravery. She woke up one day and realized there was a Hitler inside her. Realize the darker side and do something with it ... I'm still struggling ... Animals and loving them are there ... Carol Chessman in the 50's, active in vigils around the death penalty ... I am very upset with God's wrath, vengeance: What do I do with that in my Jewish background?"

I was stunned, along with others, with the way we had created in a few short minutes a powerful personal history of non-violence and civil disobedience. This was our collective history. For us it was real.

There were, quite naturally, a number of rituals connected with our Good Friday demonstration, beginning with an ecumenical Holy Thursday service after our day of training, culminating in an Easter morning Eucharist in the desert. Each contained a lesson for me so powerful I was thoroughly unprepared for what occurred. It was as though the planners of these rituals knew in advance my innermost thoughts and feelings. I was delighted with the creativity of people--- mimes, dancers, musicians, speakers. Though there were many clergy, (more than I realized at the time) they in no way dominated the ceremonies. How different this experience was from the Maundy Thursday service at my church in New York City where I would be watching a Bishop, representing Jesus, wash the feet, (actually one foot) of twelve persons chosen from the parish family. Yet here in Nevada I would be missing the intense drama of that other service which culminates, after the alter has been stripped of all ornamentation and scrubbed with vinegar, in the priest and choir suddenly running from the church as the lights are extinguished. This dramatic act symbolizing the people's abandonment of Jesus before his crucifixion, never fails to send sharp stabs of pain into my heart and gut. None of that would happen here, I was certain.

Here in Nevada, several bowls of water were placed around the room and at one point we were invited to take turns washing and drying one another's hands. When it came my turn to have my hands washed, the man who performed the rite gazed at me with gentle, compassionate eyes conveying much wisdom. The next day I discovered he was a Bishop! In the past, in New York I had wondered if I would ever be chosen to have this ceremonial washing by a Bishop. "Not likely", speculated my stony self. Yet it had happened. I had come to Nevada and without knowing it, been chosen. Once again, the stony aloofness dissolved, this time by feelings of deep gratitude.

When the Nevada service was over, a spaghetti supper appeared, served by volunteers. As I sat with people I didn't know, I listened to them tell what had brought them to this place.

Then suddenly, the coordinator of our New York group appeared saying, "I'm leaving now and the rest have already gone." I was caught completely by surprise. So busy had I been meeting new people, I failed to notice that my buddies were no longer present.

Without warning, I felt abandoned, not because they had left, rather because they had left without *telling me.* I'm familiar with that feeling and understand its source. Because my mother had died quite suddenly when I was four years old, I panic when people, (as I had experienced her leaving) go away without telling me where they're going. I've now learned how to process this feeling and comfort myself so that it's quickly released. But it wasn't until much later that I connected that feeling of abandonment with the abandonment of Jesus by his friends before his trial and crucifixion. There in Nevada, I was no longer a spectator of the Passion, albeit an involved one, I had become one of the players.

Repeatedly in the next three days, I had the disconcerting experience of being one of the original disciples of Jesus during the events that led up to his death and resurrection. Each time I was unprepared for the intensity of my response.

On Good Friday we arose at 4:30 in the morning to be at the entrance to the test site by 6:30. When we arrived, we stood in silence for an hour and a half along both sides of a road just off a main highway, watching people in cars, busses and trucks stream past on their way to work at the test site. Majestic gray mountains loomed up in the distance to our left and right. Between these natural boundaries lay desert, dotted by cactus, laced by barbed wire fence. I thought, "Nothing I do or say will change any of this." The message from my surroundings mirrored that of the Departments of Energy and Defense.

They were all saying, "Your thoughts, feelings and actions are truly insignificant and futile."

More recently I made a second trip to the same Nevada test site to commemorate Hiroshima Day and once again get arrested. My feelings of personal helplessness and hopelessness in the face of overwhelming forces were, if anything, stronger. Yet, in no way is this to suggest discouragement or a lessoning of my involvement. Rather I realized my need to summon up further resources to increase my commitment to making peace. Not knowing the form this would take, I recognized I needed to make a profound personal effort and sacrifice if I were to help bring about a shift from a consciousness which believes that security (individual as well as group) lies in manufacturing the tools of violence and destruction rather than building a strong network of interdependence and diversity with the tools of cooperation and trust. This newer awakening was not yet apparent on that Good Friday morning when I was still innocent, caught up in my initial part in a powerful event.

Our silent vigil by the side of the road ended as we gathered in the nearby desert for the commemoration of the Way of the Cross. This liturgy, familiar in various forms to Christians throughout the world, reenacts Jesus' journey with the cross from Jerusalem to Calvary. In the past, I had avoided this service, considering it too gloomy for my tastes. This Way of the Cross would be different, I sensed, though I had no way of knowing what lay in store. As the sun rose above the mountains to the East, and began to warm us, we gathered in a circle, about three hundred strong. An eight-foot rough wooden cross stood in the center, held in place by a young man. Mimes dressed in white and made-up in whiteface handed each of us a small piece of paper on which was written,

```
Your hope for resurrection of a personal nature
_____

Your hope for resurrection of a global nature
_____
```

We were instructed to fill in our answers and hold onto our paper. We were also asked to pick up a rock along the way and carry it with us.

Reader #1 began, "To crucify: to execute - to despair of - to get out of the way - to put in solitary - to leave an electric light on day and night - to sentence for life - to order special treatment."

Reader #2 said, "It is an official place, this pavement of judgment, even with the crowd milling around shouting for blood. It is all done according to the book, the legal niceties (such as they are) observed."

Reader #1: "Pilate went out to them and said, 'What accusation do you bring against this man?' They answered and said unto him, 'If this man were not an evildoer, we would not have delivered him up to you.' They cried out, 'Away with him, crucify him!' Pilate said to them, 'Shall I crucify your King?' The chief priests said, 'We have no king but Caesar.' So, he then delivered him to them to be crucified."

Reader #2: "But the terrible fact is, the powers that be have just pronounced a death sentence on the Life of the world. It seems a popular decision. And afterward Pilate washes his hands."

The words I had just heard were ringing in my ears, "to despair of ... to sentence for life." They were speaking to *me*!

Then one of the mimes stepped into the circle and nailed a gavel to the cross." The person holding the cross picked it up and carried it out of the circle as people parted to allow him to pass. We followed in silence to the next station about fifty feet away. When I arrived there and found a spot where I could see into the newly reformed circle, I noticed that a new person was holding up the cross.

A third reader began, "To crucify: to do away with - to destroy - to liquidate - to wipe out - to purge - to expel - to straighten out - to streamline - to urban renew - to evict - to threaten eviction - to do someone in."

From a fourth reader we heard, "The train is crowded and noisy and rides for days. We have no food. Where are we going? No one knows for certain but, all are afraid." The reader went on and ended with, "Come please with me: Sarah and Rachel, Rebecca and Ruth, Deborah and

Ester, Mothers of Israel. They cannot slaughter us all."
The mimes stepped forward and nailed a Star of David
to the cross; we moved to Station 3.

Was I the driver of the train? I felt accused.

A new person took up the cross and Reader #5
continued. "To crucify: to send to a state welfare home -
to turn into a criminal - to encourage dependency - to
addict - to foster neurosis - to intimidate - to stupefy - to
pull the rug from under - to cow - to brutalize." Then
came a description of the trip to Calvary, of Simon
pulled out of the crowd to carry the cross.

Mixed in with the retelling of the events of the first
Good Friday was comment on our present dilemma.
Time seemed to fall away and there was no separation
between "then" and "now".

".. . pulling splinters from his palms, Simon will not
imagine the service he has done, the place he has made
for himself in history. However unwillingly, he helped ...
when there was no help left. For this new cross there is
no help, no unwilling stranger to take the load, even for
a few last moments before the inevitable end. It belongs
to us and to our children and we must carry it alone, all
of us. Carry it... or somehow put an end to it, before it
brings the end crashing down on all of us.

"Jesus went out to the place called 'the place of the
skull' which is called in Hebrew, Golgotha. There they
crucified him, and with him two others, one on either
side and Jesus in between."

The mimes hammered three nails into the cross where the hands and feet would have been. They placed a crown of desert thorns over the top of the cross and then a new person picked it up and carried it to the next station.

As we moved from spot to spot in the desert, I noticed that in addition to the drama of the cross's journey, there was a whole other level of activity being enacted. A public address system had been set up so that everyone could hear this liturgy. Each time we changed location, a crew of people silently and skillfully picked up microphones, speakers and whatever other paraphernalia was necessary and repositioned them quickly, before fading into the crowd. Silently, I embraced these sweaty stagehands.

At station 4, the 7th Reader continued, "To crucify: to forget - to conceal - to not want to make a fuss about - to repress - to not have known about it - to consider it an isolated case - to call it inevitable - to let it happen."

Now I surely felt a great weight pressing on me. This was *my* burden; I could no longer sluff it off on others.

Reader #8: "After this, Jesus, knowing that all things had already been accomplished, in order that the Scripture might be fulfilled, said, 'I am thirsty.' "A jar full of vinegar stood there, so putting a sponge soaked in the vinegar on a hyssop stick they held it up to his mouth."

Very much as Bach and Handel in their great narrative works reenacting the Passion, the composer of this liturgy paused to deliver comment on the action. And so, Reader #7 recited:

"My God,
I thirst in the cross and from the cross.
and as one upon the cross.
My body aches in weakness.
I thirst and uranium fire bakes dry the earth
where shadows stick.
Cool, O God, my burns.
I thirst and the rain comes
bearing radiation.
I thirst and they offer a victory
of ashes in our mouths.
I thirst and they toast the launching
of a Trident with champagne.

I thirst and the military cup runneth over.
I thirst for you, O God,
and prayer goes dry in the throat.
Thirst for an end to crosses,
thirst in my heart for truth
plain and simple.
Thirst for the cup passed hand to hand
among the ones I love
(and even at the table with mine enemies).
Thirst after righteousness,
that the cup of blessing be poured out
upon the earth.
Thirst for the rolling down of overflowing
streams.
Thirst for the deep still waters of peace in
the end.
I thirst in faith
that thirst of bitter agony
for the dew of morning.
Amen."

My throat was dry and throbbing, my whole body ached. 'So, this is what it means to thirst," I thought.

One of the mimes threw a cup of vinegar over the cross and the crowd parted once again, allowing a new bearer to pass to the next station. We followed, carrying the rocks we had picked up along the way. When we reached Station 5, each of us placed our rock at the base of the cross, securing it in place so that it could stand alone. In this new space the cross was at the rim of a circle delineated by two or three rows of wooden planks on cinder blocks, making low benches. I found a place in the front row. Those who had no seat stood around and behind us. In the center of the circle was a large black box, the size and shape of a coffin. The cover was off. As I took in this scene, I was gripped with foreboding. "What next?" I wondered.

Reader #9: "To crucify: to bump off – to silence for good - to bind and gag - to deprive of language - to make deaf and dumb - to plug the ears - to put off with false hopes - to blindfold - to gouge the eyes - to turn into consumers - to blind - to stifle."

Reader #10: "When the sixth hour came, there was darkness over the whole land until the ninth hour. And at the ninth hour Jesus cried out in a loud voice, 'Eloi, Eloi, lama sabachthani?' which means, 'My God, my God, why have you forsaken me?' When some of those who stood by heard this, they said, 'Listen, he is calling for Elijah' Someone said, 'Wait and see if Elijah will come to take him down.' But Jesus gave a loud cry and breathed his last. And the veil of the Temple was torn in two from top to bottom."

Representatives of the Shoshoni Nation spoke and welcomed us to their land. They told us that the entire test site area, (100 square miles larger than the state of Rhode Island) had been part of their sacred hunting grounds never formally deeded to the U.S. Government, but given only the right of passage. To us they gave permission to go on their land and later distributed signed copies of that statement. They prayed in the Shoshoni language. Other people spoke and prayed. We sang the Negro spiritual "Were you there when they crucified my Lord?"

Just as I was beginning to bring my feelings under some semblance of control, we launched into a history of nuclear weapons since 1945, done in a litany. Readers recited event after event beginning with the first atomic test in New Mexico. In between each statement, we responded in unison with, "Forgive us, Oh Lord and help us!" It was all I could do to say those words, so large was the lump in my throat. Asking for forgiveness wasn't as hard as asking for help. Help was what I needed more than anything else in the world and like Hamlet, the word stuck in my throat.

More singing, more prayers and responses. I stumbled on with the others, tears streaming down my face, to the last station of the cross. I remember seeing Louie in his brown Franciscan habit, a magnificent, tall figure carrying the cross high, toward the place where we were to commit our acts of civil disobedience—the place where a number of uniformed marshals were waiting. The sun was hot now. Those who were planning to be arrested were asked to kneel on the rough dry ground while the others, the support team, placed their hands on our heads and shoulders and recited together a prayer of commission.

As I knelt, sharp stones pressed into my knees. In a strange way this physical discomfort was almost welcoming. At the same time, I felt the comforting presence of strangers' hands on my head and shoulders. We then reversed roles and commissioned the support team. As we moved from station to station, we sang over and over,

> We are gentle loving people
> Singing, singing for our lives.

Now the service was over but we continued singing that song. We moved into the road, took up our banner, which read, "Stop testing," with the outline of a huge dove of peace in the middle and started down toward the cattle guard. During our training we had heard a great deal about this cattle guard which is the spot on the road beyond which the Department of Energy people have decided unauthorized persons may not go. In the past protesters had been allowed to march two miles further down the road before they were stopped but the rules of this game keep changing, we were told. Hundreds of people lined the sides of the road. The singing continued,

> We are gentle loving people
> Singing, singing for our lives.

As each group went over the cattle guard and was arrested by waiting officers, the crowd cheered and clapped.

Our group of seven women, (the three others were our support team) had elected to block the road with our banner instead of trespassing, thereby creating a "public nuisance", an offense making us subject to arrest. As we moved down the road it happened that I was on the end of the line toward the center of the road. As long as we stayed on one side of the Yellow divider, the marshals would not approach us. It became my task, therefore, to step out to the left, cross the yellow line and help stretch our group across the entire road. As soon as I did that, it was like magic. The marshals approached us with a warning and then when we didn't move, they simply took each of us by the arm, led us away and placed plastic handcuffs on our wrists.

I was so involved in the emotions of the preceding service; I was unable to deal with this new event with any detachment. I felt utterly miserable, *not at being arrested,* but at the state of the world! I felt responsible for all the terrible events we had been reviewing. The reality of the crucifixion, plus all the endless acts of violence and destruction that humans have been committing ever since was more than I could bear. It was as though the mountains in the distance had come tumbling down suffocating me with their massive weight. No wonder the actual arrest seemed unreal and trivial compared to this catastrophic dilemma! I did notice the marshals were quite nervous and anxious performing their duties. They took polaroid pictures of each of us with our arresting officer for identification purposes when we were issued our citations later. When it came time for my photo, I was still buried under my mountain, consumed by heaviness and doom. Later, when we were being processed in Beatty, I had a chance to see that picture and I overheard one marshal say to another, "Here's a really grim one!" How right he was! I hardly recognized myself in the photo, so severe and black was my expression. I thought, how difficult it must be for the marshals to have to deal with someone so hostile. By the time I reached that point in my thinking I had regained much of my balance and was able to bring some lightness to the situation.

After the "photo opportunity", we climbed into waiting busses rather like children going on a school outing. As we pulled out onto the highway for the 45-mile trip to Beatty, the remaining crowd cheered and waved. My heaviness receded as I reconnected with friends and heard their stories. In spite of being handcuffed, we managed to share water from our canteens. On the surface, I appeared relaxed but deep inside I was working to repair the damage incurred during the past hour. I was still engaged in sorting out and healing my emotional self, left raw and vulnerable by the events of the morning, when we rolled into the one-horse town of Beatty and I saw Louie again. His gentle, radiating energy acted as a soothing ointment to my open wounds.

I had further opportunity to meditate on all this the following day when a small group of us returned to the vigil site in the desert. A fierce wind was blowing. Someone said they had tested another weapon, earlier that morning. We huddled together in a circle against the wind and Louie, this time without his habit, suggested we go off into the desert by ourselves and spend a time in silence. I moved toward the Western mountains climbing awkwardly up and down shallow gullies, observing the different kinds of cactus that thrive in this arid land. I sat down on an embankment trying to get out of the fierce wind. What was the meaning of this powerful blast? Its very magnitude insured my attention but what was the message? I waited, hoping an answer would come. Presently I stood up and started back. A jack rabbit with huge ears jumped in front of me and darted off to the right. He stopped about 10 yards away and sat absolutely still observing me out of the corner of his eye. I did the same. Silently I thanked him for allowing me to share his territory and wished him no harm. He made no move. Perhaps he too was waiting, waiting for something to happen.

In that brief encounter he taught me so much about waiting: it requires absolute stillness and concentration.

Back at the vigil site, we gathered again in a circle and shared our thoughts and feelings. We had to shout to be heard above the wind. I strained to listen as people spoke of sadness, waiting, anger. I told of my confusion and despair the previous day and how powerfully I had felt carried back in time. We spoke of the discomfort of not knowing what lay ahead. We were frightened and unsure. To know that others had similar feelings was itself comforting.

I went away with the picture of that jack rabbit etched in my mind. Ears up, nose to the wind, eyes unblinking, alert and waiting, totally present.

On Easter morning, I again arose very early to catch a ride back to our now familiar gathering spot. The low wooden planks were there forming a circle and in the center was the black coffin. Louie was once again wearing his simple brown robe. Mimes gave us each a balloon tied with a ribbon. They danced high in the air, a cheerful display. The wind, calmer now, had lost its angry fierceness but not its spirit. I sensed within myself and around me a new mood of quiet expectancy. Several people read Biblical passages as well as contemporary stories of Central American origin. Once again, I found time melting away, it was all happening here and now. The mimes moved about the circle clearly in search of something. They even investigated under Louie's robe while he looked on with an amused smile. Eventually a crow bar was discovered and with exaggerated motions reminiscent of the *comedia del arte*, the mimes pried off the cover of the coffin. Out floated a great bunch of brightly colored balloons all tied together. Attached at the end were the bits of paper from Good Friday, containing all our many hopes for resurrection.

Just as I had been devastated by the symbolic death of my hopes on Good Friday, now my heart all but exploded with joy as I watched the balloons carry their precious cargo aloft. They became smaller and smaller in the immense expanse of blue sky until we could see them no longer. As I looked around, I saw my surprise and delight mirrored in the faces of others. I kept looking in the direction the balloons had taken, knowing they were safely launched on their journey.

Now the coffin was transformed into an altar and draped with a white cloth. The wild flowers we had stopped to pick on our way appeared. Someone had baked a round loaf of bread. A cross and a large goblet of wine were there. Then very simply, Louie reenacted the celebration of the Last Supper. We joined in with prayers and singing. The bread and wine were passed around the circle. Toward the end, Louie suggested we release our individual balloons to the sky along with a few words as an offering of thanksgiving. As I let go of my balloon, I thanked all the people who had helped and supported me in coming on my Journey. I felt their presence around me as I acknowledged their contribution. At that moment I knew the journey had only just begun.

TWELVE

Exploring East Africa

Ever since I was eighteen years old, I have, from time to time, felt powerfully pulled toward some activity or teacher, without knowing why. It is only after fully engaging with the person, project or process, sometimes years later, that the reasons behind that urgent directive become clear. Occasionally I have willfully resisted or denied that strong urging and in those cases, invariably I have found myself smacked down in no uncertain terms. It is as though suddenly I find myself flat on my face in the mud.

A good example of this phenomenon occurred when I felt strongly pulled to join an Earth Watch research team in Zimbabwe the summer of 1989. Along with a compelling attraction toward this project on Health and Nutrition, was the intention to spend time traveling *on my own* in Africa after the project ended. Having lived alone in New York City for over twelve years at this point, I was used to traveling solo but usually my trips entailed either joining a group or visiting family or friends. This time, I made a commitment to myself to incorporate a solo tour of parts of East Africa. At the time, I remember this decision felt rather scary. I had friends who had spent a lifetime of traveling widely on their own and they seemed to have thrived but still it felt very foreign to my life experience. It felt risky, not unlike deciding to join a nudist colony. The prospect made me feel exposed and vulnerable without the safety of a group. Would I be able to make it on my own, I wondered?

While all those doubts and fears were rattling around in my head and gut, I went ahead, researched different parts of East Africa, signed up with Earth Watch, booked my flight, and eventually found myself in a small town south of Harare sharing a modern suburban house for two weeks with a bunch of US women, plus two Zimbabweans: The Chief Investigator and her male assistant. The research project entailed our visiting some of the many health clinics that existed at that time throughout the country to interview young women with at least one child two years old or younger to collect information about their diet. Each of us had a young interpreter, though some of the women we interviewed spoke English. We were given extensive questionnaires to fill out during our interviews. The purpose of the research was to discover what these women were eating themselves and what they were feeding their children. The results were eventually presented to the Zimbabwean Ministry of Health. In addition to the clinic visits, we asked certain of the women if we might make a home visit. Two days a week we spent several hours with them, usually sharing a meal. I thoroughly enjoyed the entire process.

In the evenings, we would return to our suburban home, sit around the dining room table or in the living room talking about our experiences and getting to know one another. The first night, I discovered that one of the women, Marge, had been a year ahead of me in the Theatre Department at Smith College. Since we hadn't seen one another for 38 years and both of us had acquired new last names, we had not made the connection. After a couple of days, I discovered another one of our team, I'll call her Ruth, was also planning to travel on her own after our two-week Earth Watch stint ended. Ruth and I discussed the various spots that we each were planning to visit and found that many of them were the same. After further discussion, we agreed to hook up and travel together.

As the days went by, however, a voice in my head

wondered, "Is Ruth going to be a compatible traveling companion?" I dismissed the questioner and continued to forge on with our joint plan.

A couple of days before our nutrition project was over, Ruth came to me and asked, "I'm wondering if it's a good thing for us to travel together. I'm not sure we would get along." Just as I had dismissed the doubting voice in my own head, so I pooh-poohed Ruth's concern with, "It'll be just fine."

At the conclusion of our two weeks, we all returned to Harare and the same small, pleasant hotel where we had first met upon our arrival. The plan was for Ruth and me to secure flights, train tickets and reservations to some of the prime sights in Zimbabwe, then continue on to Malawi and finally Kenya. I took care of these tasks, cashed in some American Express travelers' checks and having time before the overnight train to Victoria Falls, I went to the park in the center of Harare to sit on the grass, munch on a sandwich, and read my book, with my backpack at my side. There were a number of Zimbabweans near me doing just that, some of them in business attire, perhaps on their lunch hour. The park was well groomed with ample beds of bright flowers and enormous tree-sized poinsettias in full bloom everywhere.

Suddenly, a man was crouching before me waving a paper in my face asking me to give money to some cause. I had been warned about these fellows and had encountered them previously on the street. They were pickpockets, I was told and to be avoided at all costs. Loudly and angrily I told this fellow to go away, gesturing with my hands. He left. Shortly thereafter, I got up to go myself. When I reached into my backpack, I discovered my wallet was gone. Not only my wallet with $100 worth of cash but my ticket back to the USA and my passport. Normally I kept these items safely in a money belt but I had taken them out that morning and placed them in my oversized wallet because I knew I would need the passport to cash travelers' checks and I had been to the airline office to adjust my return ticket.

In the next few hours, I went rapidly through Elizabeth Kubler Ross's description of the five stages of death, starting with denial ("Oh, no, this can't be true!"); anger ("I hate this place, I wish I'd never come!"); negotiation ("My wallet must be here some place, I'll look again."); resignation ("I can't go anywhere now, I'm stuck here, I have no passport."); finally to acceptance ("At least I still have the rest of my traveler checks and I can get a new copy of my ticket home. I'll go to the American Embassy and get a new passport.").

The American Embassy was less than welcoming, however, when I showed up. The fellow behind the window curtly informed me that the only way I could get a replacement passport was to come with someone who had known me for more than two years who would vouch for my authenticity. My immediate internal response was, "Now I know what it feels like to be a known criminal!" After I absorbed this unwelcome news and realized that the bored bureaucrat facing me was totally uninterested in my situation regardless of my earnest appeals, I stepped away from his window and began to think. All my life I've been a compulsive problem solver and in the early seventies I had a business called Can Do. My partner and I took on and solved other people's "impossible" dilemmas, the weirder the better.

I happened to know that Marge was still in the country. The day before, we had dropped her off and met a friend of hers, plus several family members at their house on the outskirts of Harare, where Marge was spending the weekend. I also had her host's telephone number, though I knew she was off hiking for the weekend with her friend. What's more, I knew that Marge was an attorney and had visited Zimbabwe many times in the past on business. Maybe I could pull myself out of this bottomless hole after all. Returning to my hotel, I called the house (this was in the ancient pre-cell phone days), spoke to the mother and left an urgent message for Marge to call me when she returned on Sunday evening.

That afternoon, after reporting the theft to the police, turning in my newly purchased train ticket, and dealing with the airline office, I bade farewell to Ruth as she set off with another companion for Victoria Falls.

Somewhat resigned to my situation by now, I took my book and retreated to the quiet of the hotel's walled garden.

After an hour or so, a young couple that I judged to be in their thirties, appeared obviously looking around to see what was there. They spoke to me and asked about the hotel. They had just arrived in Zimbabwe having spent a month in Kenya, then another in Malawi. Inviting them to join me, we sat talking for perhaps the better part of an hour. I explained my situation and told them that as soon as I received a new passport, I planned to visit, in reverse order, the two countries they had just left. With that, they told me everything I needed to know to find my way. It seems they had thoroughly researched inexpensive, well run and safe places to stay in both Malawi and Kenya. They described these places and gave me the names and addresses plus the location of a very reasonable camping safari company out of Nairobi. All this information came pouring out in rich detail, plus suggestions of how to find my way to these places. Needless to say, I took grateful notes realizing as I did, that these two generous Canadians were handing me a precious gift. Now I knew I would be all right on my own. Then they vanished and I never saw them again. I never even discovered their names.

Marge phoned me on Sunday evening, and I told her my predicament. We met at the Embassy first thing on Monday morning, where we were immediately ushered into the Consul's office. It turns out that the two were old friends, having done business together for several years. The Consul was highly amused at our story of having unexpectedly reconnected after so many years. She signed the necessary papers, the first essential step towards procuring a new passport.

For the next two weeks I found my way to all the places the Canadians had described. Their advice proved reliable, I had adventures galore along the way including a bout of malaria, but I survived. It wasn't until I boarded the plane to come home and had plenty of time to mull over my entire trip that I fully realized the implications of all that had transpired.

THIRTEEN

Traditional Community

In May of 2006, I traveled to Bali to attend a Global Healing conference and host an all-day workshop. After the conference, I stayed on for several days to explore the island, as well as the next island to the east, Lombok. There I found an English-speaking guide to drive me to see the island's natural and cultural spots of interest. On the afternoon of my third day there, returning from visiting a spectacular waterfall, he asked me, "Would you like to visit a traditional village?" "Oh, yes!" I eagerly responded. The guide explained that he knew the head man of the village and for a small sum of money he had permission to occasionally take tourists to visit.

On our way there, my guide told me that these people were farmers, growing and raising all the food they needed to sustain themselves, with enough left over to sell at the local market so that they had money to pay the modest school fees for their children. In addition to their vegetable gardens, they raised chickens and goats.

When we arrived, I saw about ten small houses clustered together. There were no people about, but my guide told me it was OK to enter one of the houses. Inside the doorway I found a simple kitchen—sink, counter space, a few cooking utensils and dishes—with everything neatly in place. Beyond was the sleeping area consisting of two pairs of double-decker bunks. I realized that here in the tropics, life was lived outdoors and shelter was mainly used for preparing meals and sleeping. Emerging from my brief inspection of this orderly and extremely modest little dirt-floored dwelling, I looked around wondering where the people were. In the distance I could see fields planted with different crops. Nearby to my left were several chickens and a few goats wandering about. Hearing laughter, I glanced to my right down a gentle incline and spotted a cluster of about thirty people. As we approached, I could see they were adults and children of all ages intently focused in some kind of activity. Drawing closer, I saw they were playing with small wooden tops, set in motion by lengths of wound up string. It was the age-old game of seeing whose top could spin the longest by bumping into another top and knocking it out of play. The entire village was enjoying this pastime. Both adults and some of the children greeted us cordially, and though we had no language in common, they drew me into the fun by eagerly showing me how the tops worked. As the game continued, I noticed that a few of the children kept running over to a nearby platform structure not far away. In Indonesia, one sees these structures frequently—in the rice fields and other places where people gather outdoors. They're about the size of a four-poster double bed, only square, raised off the ground about three feet and with a straw roof overhead. Called a "Lumbund", people use these structures to get out of the hot sun (or rain) when they're working, as well as a way for the elderly to join in the community activities. There was someone reclining in this structure. When I walked over to investigate, I discovered the occupant was an elderly woman. It seems the children were keeping her updated on how the top game was progressing—whose top was able to keep spinning the longest. She obviously welcomed these bulletins from, I presumed, her great grandchildren. After greeting her and asking a few questions (translated by my guide), I ventured to ask her how old she was. Through my guide, she replied, "I'm not sure, but I think ninety-two." As we drove away, I remember thinking to myself, "Now, there's a truly happy community."

That visit – brief though it was – has stayed with me over the years, reminding me that what I'd glimpsed that afternoon constituted the essential elements of any healthy community, regardless of size or place in the larger society. That small group of Indonesians had chosen to live in such a way that had as integral parts of its daily routine a combination of work and play, which included all members regardless of age or disability.

While, no doubt there are similar communities existing today in other parts of the world, they are largely unknown to the vast majority of people living in what we are pleased to call more "civilized" societies. In today's Western civilization, there is scant acknowledgement of happiness as a central, essential value. Even though Thomas Jefferson, near the beginning of the Declaration of Independence, states that one of our "unalienable Rights" is "the pursuit of Happiness," in modern times, for so many, happiness has become equated with financial wealth. Couple this belief with a vision of eternal youth and beauty and you have a quick sketch of today's popular culture. What's more, we're all aware of the extent to which many people in the last years of their lives are segregated into "senior" communities— out of sight, out of mind.

Obviously, we're not going to dismantle our complex modern societies to emulate a tiny community on a small, insignificant island in the Indian Ocean. It might be fruitful, however, to take a good look at today's world, noticing the overwhelming sense of instability, coupled with high-grade anxiety and other forms of fear that permeate public and private discourse globally. What our Indonesian brothers and sisters showed me that day, by the choices they had made, was that a stable community thrives when *everyone* regularly contributes to the life of the whole. And that whole requires balanced portions of both work and play. By including their elders, they acknowledge the intrinsic and inextricable love-filled partnership of life and death.

FOURTEEN

Rock-Throwing Party

While taking an afternoon walk along the Hudson River one afternoon in August of 2016, I got to thinking about people's funerals and wakes. "It's not *fair!*" my mind complained. "All sorts of family and friends show up to celebrate the life of their relative or dear friend, but the person who's died isn't *there* to enjoy the story-telling!" I continued to walk for a bit and think about this knotty problem. Then out of nowhere, came this plan. "*I'm* going to have *my* wake *before* I die! I'll invite family and friends to gather so we can *all* enjoy sharing memories." Very pleased with this idea, I continued on my walk, fleshing out the details of such an event.

Then, later that year on December 15, while having lunch with two friends, I had a seizure, lost consciousness and was taken by ambulance to Mt Sinai Hospital, where they plugged me into several life-sustaining devices. My four children were notified and Peggy volunteered to come up to NYC from Carrboro, NC to show the Mt Sinai doctor my Living Will, which stated that I did not want to be kept alive by artificial means. At this point everyone, including the attending physician, assumed I was in the process of dying. It took considerable searching but when Peggy finally found my Living Will, she took it up to Mt Sinai and showed it to the doctor. Since it was an authentic, official document, he followed my wishes and directed the nurses to unplug the devices to which I was attached. The result was—I woke up.

In a day or two, no longer needing acute care, I was moved to a rehab facility overlooking the East River. By this time, Louise had managed to return from France. Instead of attending my funeral, she found me sitting up and taking nourishment. The next day, she brought me some clothes from my apartment and we took off for a couple of brief adventures. The nearby new East Side subway had recently opened, so we took a ride for a few stops to check it out. Another day, we took the equally close aerial tram over the East River to Roosevelt Island, wandered around a bit and then returned to the rehab place. When Louise had first lived in Jackson Hole, Wyoming, she had operated a similar aerial tram that carried skiers to the mountain top, so she especially enjoyed riding in an urban tram.

After five days, I was allowed to go home with anti-seizure pills to take twice a day for the rest of my life. My kids, having consulted with one another by phone, felt I should no longer live alone. Louise researched Senior Residences in New Hampshire, not far from my son Paul in eastern Vermont. She and I rented a car and drove up in early January to visit three of these facilities. I chose the one in Keene. We returned to NYC and set to work clearing out lots of stuff I would no longer need, such as the contents of several bookcases of books. Seven boxes full of hard-cover books went to the local Public Library and three boxes of paperbacks went to Brooklyn to be delivered to prisons.

As I looked around my three-room apartment, I realized that over the years, during my travels, I'd collected lots and lots of rocks from different parts of the world.

"What am I going to do with all these rocks?", I asked Louise. I can't take *rocks* to New Hampshire! It's the *Granite* State!"

"When I left Jackson last year, I took all my rocks to the nearby Snake River and threw them in, returning them to nature."

"Well, I've got the *Hudson River* only two blocks away!" I replied.

Going to my computer, I typed up an invitation that

began with, "You are invited to a Rock-Throwing Party." The details of when and where followed. This email invitation went to about 18 friends and relations in and around NYC. On the appointed afternoon, twelve people showed up. As planned, Louise and I met them at a statue on Riverside Drive and 89th Street with a cart full of rocks. We proceeded down to the path that runs above the river on the west side of Manhattan, unpacked a large bundle of rocks which I lined up in a long row along the sturdy wooden rail on the river-side of the path.

"Now, *your* job is to pick out a rock that especially appeals to you, then, either silently or with a simple spoken wish, respectfully return it to nature." A couple of rock lovers were so taken with a particular rock, they pounced on it, asking if they could take it home with them.

"That's OK with me, just don't try to give it back to me if you tire of it," was my reply. People walked up and down the path, inspecting the rocks carefully. Then, one by one, they each took their choice and threw it into the Hudson. I noticed, as this process continued, it acquired the feeling of a ceremony. There were enough rocks so that everyone, including Louise and I, had a chance to repeat this ritual more than once. When all the rocks had been returned to nature, I invited everyone to join me for some refreshments that Louise had prepared to complete our Rock-Throwing Ceremony.

Back at 201 West 89th Street, Louise had prepared an ample supply of corn chowder, corn bread, mulled cider and red wine. Everyone helped themselves and found a seat in my living room. Up until this point, Louise and I had carefully planned out the details of the afternoon. What followed, was wholly spontaneous.

Without prompting from me, one by one, each person started telling of an experience, a memory or project that they had shared with me at different times in the past. Here are a few samples.

Anders spoke of the magic we had created in co-producing "Tree Friends": a program that featured some of his magnificent tree portraits of a few of the world's most astonishing trees, accompanied by actor and musician friends reciting or performing tree poetry.

Aaron recalled how grateful he was when I invited him to come over from Brooklyn for dinner shortly after his father had married my daughter, Peggy. He realized I was welcoming him into a new family.

Debbie cherished the many events, projects and cutting-edge speakers FIONS had hosted when we both had been active in following the inspiration of Apollo 14 Astronaut, Edgar Mitchell, who, after returning from the Moon, had founded the Institute of Noetic Science (IONS), to use science to explore consciousness.

Richard talked of the many walks we took together in Central Park, enjoying the urban flora and fauna, as well as the great conversations on a variety of wide-ranging topics. In addition, as a Mentor for the FIONS program, Teens for Planet Earth, he enjoyed helping some of the teams of high-schoolers transfer their ideas about improving the environment into posters for a contest to be chosen for display in the NYC Transit bus/subway system.

Joanie was grateful for our many years of sharing the magnificent music and liturgy at St. Thomas Church, as well as the friendship it fostered.

After everyone departed, I sat reflecting on the events of the afternoon. Suddenly, I realized that what had occurred, was in essence, what I had envisioned the previous August: I had hosted my own wake.

True magic constructed of pure love.

Acknowledgements

A number of people have contributed to this memoir by lending a hand with technical, editorial and design issues. My great thanks go to my granddaughter, Emily Jane Wipper and my good friend, Frank Bequaert, for their help with transcribing many of the photos.

I am also grateful to those who agreed to read the manuscript prior to publication and offer their generous endorsements: Dan Hall, Richard Schiffman, Elsa Worth, Rudolph Fedrizzi and Debbie Lawrence.

Most especially, I profoundly appreciate the ongoing support and wise guidance from my daughter, Louise Gignoux. She has been my number one helper all the way. Even though Louise resides in France's Loire Valley and I am in southwestern New Hampshire, our frequent and extended phone calls keep us connected and give me the much-needed confidence to share some of these tales. There is considerably more involved in publishing a memoir than sitting down and sharing a bunch of memories: that's the relatively easy part. Where I'm especially grateful to Louise is for her cheerfully taking on the task of skillfully completing the editing forms my publisher, iUNIVERSE, requires. What's more, Louise is always there with comforting, calming and encouraging words when I lose my focus and whine, "I'm too *old* for this nonsense!"

Permissions from Copyright Holders to use certain photographs

Front Cover – Schoodic Point – Downeast Thunder Farm – Susan Bennett

The Cathedral of St. John the Divine, aerial photo of the Close, page 17 – Wayne Kempton, Cathedral archivist

The Cathedral Choir School photo, 1940, page 28 – Wayne Kempton, Cathedral archivist

Journey to Nevada photo, page 133 – attribution, *Nevada Desert Experience*

Printed in the United States
By Bookmasters